BOLD TRACKS

THIRD EDITION

Teaching Adaptive Skiing

Hal O'Leary, psia, nhs

DIRECTOR, NATIONAL SPORTS CENTER FOR THE DISABLED

Winter Park, Colorado

Third Edition 1994

Library of Congress Cataloging-in-Publication Data
O'Leary, Hal.
    Bold tracks: teaching adaptive skiing / Hal O'Leary. — 3rd ed.
        p.   cm.
    "Published in cooperation with the National Sports Center for the
Disabled, Inc." — CIP t.p. verso.
    Includes bibliographical references (p.) and index.
    ISBN 1-55566-114-9
    1. Skiing for the handicapped — Study and teaching — United States.
I. Title.
GV854.33.O54   1994
796.93'02408 — dc20   94-38281
                                                        CIP

WARNING
Skiing is a dangerous activity and should be done only with qualified instruction, proper equipment, and one's own common sense. Instructors, students and others using this manual are reminded that they participate in skiing solely at their own risk.

Published in cooperation with the
National Sports Center for the Disabled, Inc.
and generously funded in part by
the Frost Foundation and
Ski Industries of America.

Ann W. Douden, *art director, designer*
Mary M. Meinig, *writer, editor*
Betsy Armstrong, *editor*
Marjorie C. Leggitt, *illustrator*
Gus Allen Alavezos, *flipbook illustrator*
    Agent: Carol Guenzi
Gary Hall, *studio photographer*
Lori Kranz, *proofreader*
Jeanne Smith, Steve Stone. *location photographers*
Kim Thomas, Rockin' Horse Graphics,
    electronic production

Published by
Johnson Books
Boulder, Colorado

Printed in the United States of America by
Johnson Printing
1880 South 57th Court
Boulder, Colorado 80301

Cover photograph of Retta's Run, Winter Park, Colorado by Byron Hetzler. All other images by Jeff Stine. © Winter Park.

3 } CONTENTS

"You have touched us, and we have grown!"

4 } FOREWORD

I am honored to introduce someone I consider both a friend and one of the world's leading experts on recreational opportunities for individuals with disabilities. I met Hal O'Leary when I was newly disabled—I lost my leg in Vietnam in 1969. I had come with some fellow disabled veterans to Winter Park Ski Area, where Hal ran the disabled program, to participate in the U.S. Disabled Ski Championships. I came to race, party and revel in the companionship of others, like me, who were experiencing the difficulty of life with a disability.

Hal firmly believed that racers with disabilities could do anything to which they were willing to commit. Ignoring the advice of lawyers and other cautious and well-meaning souls, Winter Park organized the first challenging, one-mile-long downhill race for disabled racers. It was this kind of bone-jarring race experience that convinced me I might do better in a desk job!

So I became Executive Director of National Handicapped Sports (NHS), which funds and promotes year-round recreational and competitive opportunities for kids and adults with disabilities. Hal's program, the National Sports Center for the Disabled (NSCD), is one of 92 chapters of NHS throughout the United States that sponsors recreational and competitive programming. However, because of Hal and his outstanding staff and volunteer crew, it is the largest chapter and one of the most exemplary and innovative.

Hal's expertise is heralded worldwide. He travels all over the United States, Canada and countries abroad; makes speeches, shakes hands with important people, collects awards and listens to lots of free-flowing compliments on what a great guy he is, and so on and so on. But those who know Hal understand that accolades and awards are secondary to the satisfaction he experiences when he is teaching one young disabled child the joy of participating in skiing . . . and in life.

Recreation can provide the motivation and self-esteem that encourage children and adults with disabilities to expect only the best in life. Hal understands this instinctively and has never wasted a second thinking about a student's " limitations." For he knows, all too well, that plenty of others will tell disabled people about what they can't do. Hal is an acknowledged master at helping his students to focus on their abilities and on what they want to accomplish in life.

Every single day, Hal O'Leary wakes up with the belief that on this day he will open a new universe to a disabled child or adult—a universe of hope, of new possibilities, of friendship and fun. For he knows the future of disabled people is built one person at a time. I am pleased and proud to call him a colleague and leader in this effort and, most importantly, a friend.

Kirk Bauer
NHS, Executive Director

Hal's expertise is heralded worldwide. . . But those who know Hal understand that accolades and awards are secondary to the satisfaction he experiences when he is teaching one young disabled child the joy of participating in skiing . . . and in life.

Someone once said, "If God had meant us to ski, he would have given us feet with metal edges."

As every instructor knows, learning to ski is essentially mastering the use of special equipment and highly developed skills to overcome various natural difficulties.

The skier uses attachments called skis to compensate for the inadequate length of his feet.

He uses special boots as a supporting prosthesis to overcome the inadequate rigidity of his ankles.

A skier must develop skills to keep him upright against the pull of gravity.

When you consider the problems we have to overcome, we're all skiers with disabilities.

Hal O'Leary

Cale Kenney, former member of U.S. Disabled Ski Team.

INTRODUCTION

This manual is designed to be used by the people and places involved in teaching people with disabilities to ski—program developers, ski resort owners, program directors and managers, clinicians, instructors and volunteers.

The teaching core of the book covers the different techniques of skiing for people with disabilities: three track, four track, cerebral palsy, sit skiing, mono skiing, bi skiing and skiing for the developmentally disabled and the visually and hearing impaired. Other disabilities are covered by association and adaptation.

We use the American Teaching System (ATS) as the basis of our instruction and adapt it to each individual. We have included instructional material from *Strategies for Teaching American Teaching System*, as well as a synopsis of their system from the *American Teaching System: Alpine Skiing** in the resource section. Adaptive teaching techniques along with adaptive equipment form the cornerstones of our operation.

We repeat some of our major points about teaching in each of the sections for the benefit of the reader who is concentrating on a specific area or disability.

For everyone's benefit and understanding, we have added a major "medical section," where you will find definitions and explanations of the various disabilities. We have also compiled some glossaries of common and specialized terms, including skiing terminology and the language of adaptive equipment.

"We studied your program at great length—on the slopes and in the office—and liked what we saw: a unique and enviable program."

Winter 1968-69, the first year of the handicap program at Arapahoe Basin. From the collection of Mrs. Virginia McMurtry.

* Excerpts reprinted with permission of the Professional Ski Instructors of America from *Strategies for Teaching: American Teaching System*, P.S.I.A., Publishers Press, Salt Lake City, Utah. © 1987 and *American Teaching System: Alpine Skiing*, P.S.I.A., © 1993.

At Winter Park, an expert trail runs straight down the face of the mountain, called "Retta's Run." It was named for Retta Stanley, a registered nurse at Children's Hospital in Denver and a very special person in the development of the Winter Park Handicap Program. Retta's Run, enlarged to include glade and mogul skiing, has become a very prestigious run at Winter Park. I am sure that if Retta were here she would be very proud of the run we named in her memory.

In the early stages of our fledgling program, Retta worked with kids with disabilities from Children's Hospital—many of them cancer victims—at Winter Park to conquer their disabilities with the freedom of the mountain and downhill skiing. She gave generously of herself as an invaluable volunteer in the program. She was my teacher as well, contributing greatly to my education about people with disabilities. Retta taught me to have compassion instead of pity, and she emphasized dignity at all times.

Then cancer struck Retta, and she lost her leg above the knee. Having no pity for any disability, including her own, she became one of the first women three track national champions.

After battling cancer for eight years, Retta lost her life. Her strength, intelligence and compassion made a lasting impression on everyone she touched.

In Retta's memory, I dedicate this teaching manual, with great pride in what she brought to us all.

Hal O'Leary

Retta Stanley

Throughout this manual watch Retta ski by flipping the outer-right hand pages from front to back.

Recreation. It is good for everyone. But for the person with a disability, it is a significant factor in eliminating the web of obstacles that restrict this person. Skiing can mean adventure, exercise, growth, development, self-respect and independence.

Lack of mobility has always been the chief obstacle for people with disabilities. Most rehabilitation programs focus solely on regaining physical strength and range of motion, whereas sports programs use athletic participation to rehabilitate a person both physically and emotionally. This is especially true in downhill skiing. The skier's self-esteem skyrockets when he realizes that he can not only participate but can do so on an equal basis with able-bodied counterparts.

Recreation does more than build self-confidence. It also helps erase social barriers and retire myths held by society and replaces them with understanding of and sensitivity to a person's abilities. The increased mental fitness and physical coordination gained through skiing make the individual with a disability better able to be employed or to attend school on a full-time basis. Skiing can be a family-and-friends affair, bringing support and companionship to the skier.

It is an enormous delight to people with disabilities to move with speed, grace and ease though their skiing. They often say things like: "If I can do this, I can do anything," or "I love the wind in my face and the feeling of motion. The mountain does it for me." But in fact, this person has accomplished something that he perhaps never dreamed he could do. He is skiing.

Fred Tassone, Vietnam veteran and former coach for the U.S. Disabled Ski Team.

"I was able to challenge myself and experience a very important personal success which carried over into all aspects of my life."

ABOUT HAL O'LEARY

Hal O'Leary came to Colorado from Canada armed with the unlikely combination of a business degree and a desire to work outdoors. He was a salaried ski instructor at Winter Park and volunteered to help with the amputee program when it first began.

Hal had to fight for funding and support for his handicap ski program as it grew and took shape. But he was tenacious, unwilling to give up. By 1970 he was director of the program. His first manual, printed in 1973 under the title, "The Winter Park Amputee Ski Teaching System," enjoyed numerous printings and was translated into Japanese, Swedish and Spanish. By 1974, Hal was running an independent, well-established ski program, and his accomplishments—and reputation—were growing. In 1981, Hal garnered the prestigious Gold Quill Award from the national ski press for individuals who make significant contribution to the field of skiing. In 1982 the National Forest Service gave Hal his second major award for his important utilization of forest land in the interests of people with disabilities.

Hal has a natural talent for relating to each skier, on an individual basis, modifying techniques, equipment and instructional approach to the situation at hand. To his students, he has been teacher, counselor and confidant.

Today he is a self-taught but highly trained technician. He understands and articulates the disabilities he handles with the precision of a medical specialist. He excels in his understanding and use of adaptive equipment. He knows how to apply the skill of skiing to the art of human management. He is a consummate master at helping people to believe in their own abilities—and ultimately in themselves.

Hal travels across the United States, Canada and to countries abroad teaching and consulting with others about similiar programs. He has made numerous training films on teaching people with disabilities to ski. He has been a spokesman for his cause to government. In 1982, Hal wrote a ski teaching manual for the developmentally disabled, published by the national Special Olympics.

Hal O'Leary claims: "I have gotten so much more out of the program than I have put into it." He may think so, but many a skier would say it's a draw.

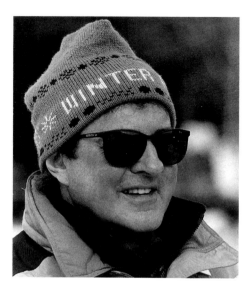

Hal O'Leary   PHOTO: BRYON HETZLER

Editor's Note: The original sports program for people with disabilites began in 1968 at Arapahoe Basin, about 50 miles west of Denver. Fifteen children from the Amputee Clinic at Children's Hospital in Denver were paired with a group of Vietnam veterans from Fitzsimons General Hospital. A "buddy system" developed that utilized the psychology of mutual support and encouragement while instructors experimented with ski techniques and equipment. Fund-raising and other program needs were handled by very committed volunteers who sought donations of all kinds locally and afar. In January 1970 the program moved to Winter Park, where our story begins. The pioneering supporters are listed in the Acknowledgments.

NATIONAL
Sports Center for the
DISABLED
WINTER PARK, CO

It began in the 1969–70 season, with 23 children from Children's Hospital in Denver, Colorado. It is now the largest and most renowned skiing program for people with disabilities in the world. It accommodates students who have one, or several, of 45 different disabilities. How did it happen? Hal O'Leary likes to tell this story.

In January 1970, Jerry Groswold, then chairman of the Board of Trustees, received a telephone call from Children's Hospital asking if Winter Park could pick up another ski area's canceled adaptive ski program. He responded to the need. The next day, ski school owner George Engel approached the group of ski instructors of Winter Park, explained the situation and asked for volunteers. "Mine was the only hand that went up," Hal explains. Hal O'Leary was then a six-year veteran ski instructor from Canada.

The next day George gave him a piece of paper. "Here," he said, "you're in charge."

Saturday, March 6, 1971.
Historical photo from
the collection of Mrs. Virginia McMurtry.

Hal quickly went to work. The youngsters were due in six days. He called the name on the paper—Willie Williams, a nurse at Children's Hospital—and obtained a pair of outriggers (short skis mounted to a crutch with a movable head). He took three days off from his regular job of teaching and taught himself to ski on three tracks, improvising techniques based on the American Teaching System.

The following Thursday was not a typical Colorado sun-filled day. It was gray and bleak. The wind was howling. When Hal skied into the midst of the 23 very cold amputees who were lying on the snow, some crying, he was bewildered. What to do now? From behind came a sharp voice commanding: "On your feet!" The children responded immediately. Later, Hal teased the nurse in his easygoing manner: "Willie, you could have said, 'Up on your foot,' since they only have one."

The dedication and camaraderie that developed among Willie, Hal, the volunteers and the children who came from the hospital were to last a long time, and from that time on, Hal was committed. "I saw joy on their faces when they moved on skis in a way they couldn't walk. Their motions were fluid and smooth, like regular skiers. I began to think of the value of skiing for other people with disabilities."

What began as fun and games for a few youngsters soon grew into a serious educational enterprise. With racing successes and media coverage, the program's reputation spread and demand for its services increased. Soon a volun-

"Willie" Williams, R.N., former Outpatient Coordinator of Rehabilitation and Orthopedics, Children's Hospital, Denver, 1968–1981 (left), and Carol Page, R.P.T., Coordinator, Handicapped Sports Program, Children's Hospital, Denver (right).

teer corps developed around the program, and more emphasis was placed on the design and use of adaptive equipment. Funding and independence came in time.

The ski program for people with disabilities has tremendous outreaching qualities for its students. The social and recreational benefits help build new attitudes, new confidences and new lives.

The program has created a positive effect not only on its students but also for the ski area and town of Winter Park. Many former students are now employees of the area or in the town. In Winter Park and in the program, these people are not different. They are very much in the mainstream of this mountain community. Conversely, many normal employees of Winter Park choose to volunteer in the ski program on their days off.

Through media coverage and international publicity, the program has become known around the world and spread across the United States to Canada, South America, Europe, Australia and New Zealand.

The program has demanded of itself the very best in recreational instruction in a caring, accepting atmosphere. The students respond in turn by demanding the best of themselves. Through shared effort, the self-confidence and pride come from knowing you have successfully achieved a goal.

Some specifics about the ski program follow:

Cooperation with Ski School

The regular ski school can be very helpful in the area of training in ATS as part of the required certification above, or for certification with Professional Ski Instructors of America. Generally speaking, a ski teaching program for people with disabilities needs its own teaching group because of the highly specialized adaptive instruction and equipment.

Ski Patrol: Lift Evacuation

Ski patrol needs to be aware of the disabilities with which this program works. They also need instruction in the evacuation of lifts in the event of lift failure for the sit skis, bi skis and mono skis, as well as for other disabilities.

Accidents

Due largely to the screening and evaluation of people with disabilities and the extensive training of staff and volunteers working on a one-to-one basis with the individuals, accidents occur very infrequently.

Insurance/ Liability

The National Sports Center for the Disabled is fully covered under the insurance of the Winter Park Recreation Association. If your program is not covered by your ski area, insurance may be obtained from National Handicapped Sports, provided that your program is a chapter of the national organization.

Summer Programs

For the past 13 years, there has been a very active summer program for people with disabilities. Some of the activities are: rafting on the Colorado River, hiking, backpacking, overnight camping, nature walks, alpine slide, chairlift rides, dance movement and adaptive swimming and tennis.

We also offer an extensive rock climbing program for the visually impaired, available for college credit.

Joe Reum

Adaptive skiing has many forms—each a specialty in its own right. It may be true that one gave rise to the next, but historically skiing for people with disabilities seems to have its roots in two contributing forces: accidental injury and war. While it is risky to try to pinpoint exact beginnings of a sport so tied to world events like war, the earliest information does seem to center in Europe around World War II and focuses on three track.

Through oral accounts given in Europe, the concept of "crutch skiing" originated in Switzerland. The Swiss attempted to use underarm crutches for skiing but eventually discarded this technique.

In 1942, a German named Franz Wendel was the first person to successfully enter competition for people with disabilities. After a leg amputation from a war injury in 1941, he fashioned a pair of crutches and attached them to short skis, enabling him to begin crutch skiing. By 1943 he was being recognized for his three track skiing. In Austria the sport began to spread by word of mouth. The encouragement and promotion of the sport by those who pioneered it helped others to get started. By the late 1940s, the Austrian Ski Association was financing a division for the people with disabilities and in 1947 organized demonstrations by amputee skiers at local annual races.

Concurrently, European and American personalities were involved with rehabilitation programs at army hospitals for amputees. Over these years, various attempts to develop and refine instructional techniques and, more importantly, adaptive equipment, were taking place. By the late 1950s, there was a ski school for amputees in Salzburg, Austria, and the first manuals on the techniques of amputee skiing had appeared.

By this time three track skiing had diffused by word of mouth from Europe to the United States. Again, the dedication and concern of a small group of people nurtured and kept alive the developing sport of three track skiing. Some were amputees themselves, some instructors, and at least one or two were specialists in prosthetics.

By the early 1960s, this group had acquired several pairs of outriggers from an Austrian firm and literally passed them around the country, to copy and refine. The sport traveled westward, developing practitioners in Oregon especially. In the 1962–63 ski season, America had its first certified amputee ski instructor from the United States Ski Association's Northwestern Division. Programs for skiers with disabilities were under way in the USA.

With additional outriggers in circulation, amputee ski schools began to flourish in America. By 1962 the National Amputee Skiers' Association had formed. (The name was changed to National Inconvenienced Sportsman's Association in 1972.) Today this group has many active chapters in the United States.

The Vietnam War produced regrettable casualties but also provided a boost to the general development of three track skiing. At Fitzsimons General Hospital near Denver, the need for rehabilitation of amputees, support of their morale and the presence of nearby magnificent skiing in the Colorado Rockies combined to move three track skiing to the forefront.

Mrs. Virginia McMurtry and Matthew Koldeway.

Teddy Kennedy training for Handicap National Championships at Winter Park.

In January 1968, the Children's Amputee Clinic at Denver's Children's Hospital became another contributing force by starting a ski program for people with disabilities. Starting at Arapahoe Basin, the program soon moved to Winter Park, Colorado, where it has flourished ever since.

Equipment also underwent many changes and refinements over these years, modifying outriggers many times to make them functional. Perhaps the most significant improvement was the development of the flipski. The flipski can be changed from a skiing outrigger into a crutch for walking or climbing by a hand-operated lanyard that is connected from the handle to a spring-loaded mechanism that locks the ski in either position, as desired.

It has been said that with the modern adaptive equipment, the special abilities required of a ski instructor are: (1) a technical knowledge of the mechanics of skiing; (2) adequate knowledge of the disability and (3) the ability to combine these for maximum efficiency in each unique situation for each individual's benefit. The new outlook that is offered the people with disabilities through skiing goes beyond increased mobility. It is physical and psychological access to "normal" activity.

Today, adaptive ski associations participate in ski races and competitions around the world—most notably the Canadian Association for Disabled Skiing, with groups in several provinces and an Annual Canadian International Disabled Ski Meet. The Handicapped Skiers Association of Japan holds similar competitions annually. Other countries that have programs for skiers with disabilities include Norway, France, Italy, Czechoslovakia, Yugoslavia and New Zealand.

From the beginning, when Franz Wendel became the first successful competitor with a disability, competition has been the natural outgrowth of programs. But the personal desire for achievement, a love of skiing and the concern of an international network of dedicated persons have made it all happen.

UPDATE . . . The major trend in three track skiing has been to extend the use of outriggers to an increasing variety of disabilities. There are now more four trackers than any other type of adaptive skier, and sit skiing is increasing in popularity. Advances in equipment have contributed to this trend.

In 1974 the ski bra was discovered in a ski show. Today the ski bra is standard equipment for the person who does not have control of his legs. But even using the ski bra, some people had trouble keeping their legs from "scissoring." In 1975 came a device called the toe spreader—a bar that fits under the bindings and across the skis with ball bearings on either end. In 1976, the slant board was developed for people who lack flex in their lower limbs and knees. This board is inserted under the bindings to give a forward or backward slant to the person's stance on the skis. "Ski legs," designed for use by below-the-knee amputees, are prostheses with the forward lean built into the leg.

Most three trackers agree that the outrigger is most useful for its stability in racing, and in the 1970s the outrigger was refined for speed and efficiency—longer and heavier in the ski tip and shorter in the shaft.

MATTHEW KOLDEWAY, 9, LONGMONT, COLO., WAS ENCOURAGED BY CAPT. RON MORRISON, FORT ATKINSON, WIS.

War, Peace Amputees Learn To Ski on Colorado Slopes

ARAPAHOE BASIN, Colo. — (AP) — Army Capt. Ron Morrison buckled a ski on the one leg he brought back from Vietnam and set off down the snow-swept slope.

A dozen other soldiers, each minus a leg, followed suit. And a like number of children, each gliding on one ski, did likewise.

"It means a lot to get a chance at being people again," said Morrison, 28, Fort Atkinson, Wis., who was wounded twice in Vietnam before a booby trap in the Mekong Delta took his right leg last August 13.

IT WAS AN EFFORT to provide this chance that fostered a learn-to-ski program for Morrison and about 20 other amputees — nearly all Vietnam combat veterans — at the Army's Fitzsimons General Hospital in Denver.

Across town at the same time, Denver Children's Hospital was setting up similar therapy for 18 children who had lost legs either through accident or congenital defect.

Then Col. Paul W. Brown, who set up the Fitzsimons program, and Dr. William J. Shinek, who organized it at Children's Hospital, got together and combined their efforts. Now the men and boys make the weekly trip to Arapahoe Basin ski area together.

"I came up here to have a good time."

don't care if I never learn to ski," Morrison said.

But he and his friends are learning.

PROGRESS OF the amputee students has astonished their volunteer instructors at the Willy Schaeffler Ski School.

They figured to keep the amputees on the practice slope for the first four weeks. All were riding the chairlift by the second trip; some made it the first time.

Two soldiers, never on skis until the amputee lessons began, did so well they took their girl friends the next time to teach them.

Most of the amputees were able to navigate a 15-pole slalom race without falling after one or two lessons.

They use an outrigger-type arrangement to stabilize themselves and maintain control. Instead of ski poles, the amputees use poles with very short skis mounted on the ends. Retractable spikes, which can be extended through the stabilizer skis into the snow, are used for walking. The spikes are retracted

THE DOUBLE amputees deserve an adapting slalom, a special one, competing using skis instead of wheels. One has been using an outrigger pulled by another skier.

Historical clipping from the collection of Mrs. Virginia McMurtry.

The material in this history was adapted from a research paper, "The History and Development of Three Track Skiing," prepared by Betty Lessard in satisfaction of course work at Michigan State University in June 1976.

"Update" adapted from a paper by Cale Kenney, January 1983.

The most radical adaptation of skiing for people with a disability came in 1978 with the advent of the "pulk," a cross-country sled for paraplegics. In 1980 the Arroya, designed for alpine skiing, became part of the national games. The "sit ski," the Arroya's generic name, has been improved on since.

The growth of adaptive skiing in the United States is reflected in the Handicap Nationals, begun at Winter Park in 1972. In 1978 a freestyle event was added. In 1979 blind skiers were allowed to race alpine, and in 1980 Arroya competition began. Then in 1982 a system of regional qualifiers was adopted to manage the greater number of competitors.

Editor's Note: The Handicap Nationals held at Winter Park between 1972 and 1981 are now moved around the country on a yearly basis. Winter Park not only hosted the 1989 Nationals, but also the 1990 World Disabled Ski Championships. This was the first time these games were held in North America.

Susan Hildebrecht, cerebral palsy, instructor.

PHOTO: STEVE STONE

Skiers of all abilities may now race in their local chapter or regional race to classify. "A" racers go on to the national championships. The highly competitive nature of this regional format promises to field athletes of higher and higher caliber for international competition.

The United States hosted a team to the Second Winter Olympic Games for people with disabilities in Geilo, Norway, in 1980. At the World Games in Switzerland in 1982, for the first time additional categories of adaptive skiing were opened to competition, including four track and blind.

Adaptive sports catapulted into a new era in 1983 when the International Olympic Committee fully sanctioned the Third World Winter Games for the Disabled. Olympic sanction was a major breakthrough not only in prestige, but it also propelled fund-raising efforts and program development worldwide. In October of that same year, a 24-member "demonstration team" chosen from selected handicap classifications was invited to participate in a demonstration at the Winter Olympic Games in Sarajevo, Yugoslavia.

Chris Lind, 1970

The Third World Winter Disabled Ski Championships were held in 1986 at Salen, Sweden. The United States team, representing a wide and highly capable range of skiers with disabilities, placed first.

Demonstrations of competition for skiers with disabilities were included at the 1988 Winter Games in Calgary, Alberta, Canada. In 1992, the IOC decided to schedule these events as bona fide Olympic medal events.

Sit skier Marilyn Hamilton   PHOTO: R.J. WALKER

TEACHING METHODS

The adaptive teaching methods presented in the following chapters for people with disabilities were derived from the American Teaching System. The first chapter, "Teaching: Two Track/ATS,"* illustrates teaching techniques for people with no disabilities. These techniques have set the stage and foundation for teaching adaptive skiing. The American Teaching System (ATS) continues to be refined and developed by the educators of the Professional Ski Instructors of America. For a synopsis of the system, see an excerpt from the *American Teaching System: Alpine Skiing,** on page 168.

The person with a disability has very special needs. They can lack balance, lateral control of the legs and hips, or have side effects of medications, spinal cord injury, emotional and behavioral problems, leg length discrepancies, skiing with prosthetic limbs, visual and hearing impairments or lack of stamina, to name a few.

In addition to dealing with the impairments caused by the disability, the disabled individual utilizes adaptive equipment that enables the person to ski. For those whose involvement requires stabilization of the skis, fore and aft, and/or the use of outriggers, the necessary adaptive equipment imposes certain restrictions. Often those particular individuals do not always have the advantage of experiencing the beginning techniques that other skiers experience, such as walking, climbing or stemming movements.

Two track, therefore, gives a basic progression of techniques to follow. Some steps may have to be deleted or enhanced, depending on the individual.

The adaptive ski instructor normally works on a one-to-one basis as opposed to in a class setting because the necessity for a wide range of adaptive equipment and techniques makes it almost impossible to work with more than one individual at a time.

* Excerpts reprinted with permission of the Professional Ski Instructors of America from *Strategies for Teaching: American Teaching System*, P.S.I.A., Publishers Press, Salt Lake City, Utah. © 1987 and *American Teaching System: Alpine Skiing,* P.S.I.A., © 1993.

Pat Campanello, instructor, teaching one-on-one   PHOTO: R.J. WALKER

Beginning Through Wedge Turns

Introduce the student to the mountain environment and safety.
Orient the student to the equipment. Introduce basic maneuvers: walking, stationary turning, turning while walking and climbing.

Getting Started

Begin on the flat.
The ideal beginner area should be well groomed and packed.
For gliding, move to a gentle slope. It is not possible in every ski area but pick terrain that allows the student to ski to a stop.
Match student's skill to the terrain.

Terrain and Conditions

Mechanics

Apply the basic skills.
Develop an awareness of controlling pressure in walking and climbing exercises, controlling edging in climbing and gliding wedge exercises, and controlling turning in the gentle gliding wedge turn.
Establish a gliding relationship between skis and snow.
Emphasize skills equally.

Introduce basic walking steps. When doing self-propelling movements, we suggest that poles be used by adult students but that they not be used by children. Pole swing and position of the basket or end of the pole should be shown in relationship to stride.

Walking

Do turning steps by stepping the tail around (pivot around the tip), then by stepping the tip around (pivot around the tail). Do them in both directions.

Turning Steps

Begin with a side step. Emphasize the need for the ski to be across the fall line, edging movements and pressure control movements. Little steps support good edge contact and help maintain balance.

Climbing Steps

SKILLS APPLICATION

Pressure Control Movements

Emphasize in walking and climbing maneuvers.

Edging Movements

Emphasize in climbing maneuvers.

Rotary Movements

Emphasize in turning steps, gliding wedge turns, wedge turns.

Balancing Movements

Emphasize in the introduction of all basic maneuvers.

Gliding Movements
Movements for which the primary motive force is external (gravity).

Straight Run Seek a comfortable position with the feet slightly apart and the joints of the body gently flexed. Students should be able to ski to a comfortable stop. If this is not possible in your area, use a side hill approach instead of a straight downhill run.

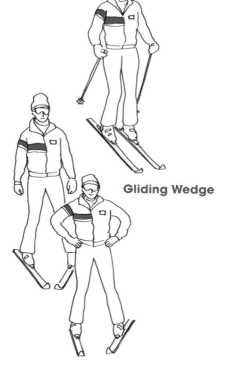

Gliding Wedge From a comfortably high stance (the hips are centered and the body is supported on the skeletal structure rather than by muscular effort) the tails of the skis are pressed slightly apart. The tips are together, and there is little, if any, edge angle between the ski and the snow. (Those who have little difficulty pressing to a wedge can ski it with the hands relaxed at the side. Others should place the hands on the hips. The ideal situation for students at this stage of development is to be without poles, but if they cannot get back up the hill or need the poles for balance, they should be given to them.)

Wedge Change Ups This maneuver strengthens the ability to move easily to a comfortable wedge position. From the straight run, the skis are gently brushed into a gliding wedge. After gliding a few feet, the skier rises slightly and allows the skis to run together. This exercise should be repeated several times. Initially the student may only be able to go from a straight run to a wedge. With practice the student will be comfortable going from the straight run to the wedge and back again several times.

Gliding Wedge Turns From a straight gliding wedge both skis are gently guided in the direction you wish to go. (No effort is made to edge or pressure the skis.) Both legs are turned in the desired direction of travel. A high body position is maintained with the hips centered. This turn should be kept very close to the fall line and will initially consist of no more than a slight deflection from the original line of travel (A). Follow the first turn by gentle deflection out of the fall line in two directions (B) and then link several turns (C). Many instructors find the first gliding wedge is accomplished by simply looking in the desired direction of travel.

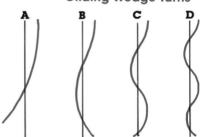

A   B   C   D

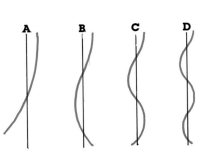

Though we call this a gliding wedge turn, as more belly is added to the turn (D) the components of controlling pressure braking become more active in the turn.

Remember that these maneuvers do not have to start in the fall line. Starting at a slight diagonal to the fall line makes the first turn easier to start.

Braking Wedge

The hips are maintained in a central position, but the tails of the skis are brushed out far enough to create significant edge angles between the ski and the snow. This requires greater muscle control than the gliding wedge and should not be practiced until the gliding wedge is mastered or the terrain and conditions require it.

> **Braking Movements**
> Movements that counteract natural motive forces to slow down or decelerate (internally generated).

Wedge Turns

From a medium-width wedge begin by turning the legs in the desired direction of travel. Keep the skis turning until they have passed beyond the fall line. Edge angle and pressure increase on the ski as the ski crosses the fall line, but this should not be emphasized.

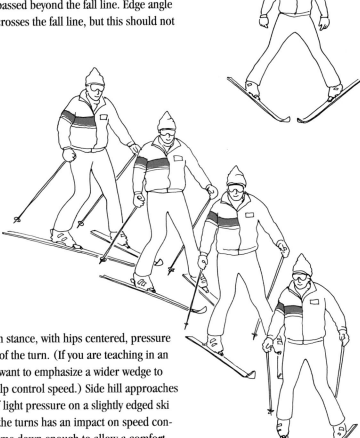

When the skier maintains a comfortably high stance, with hips centered, pressure and edge increase naturally toward the end of the turn. (If you are teaching in an area where the snow is quite hard, you will want to emphasize a wider wedge to provide snow edge relationships that will help control speed.) Side hill approaches to encourage control through application of light pressure on a slightly edged ski can be helpful. Also, changing the shape of the turns has an impact on speed control. The hip must stay centered and only come down enough to allow a comfortable wide wedge.

Wedge Turn to Wedge Christy

Introduce the students to and help them become comfortable with the dynamics of skiing (feel the forces generated by a body in motion and begin to work with them). Strengthen rotary movement skills (directing the skis by controlling turning). Emphasize two-legged steering. Develop the student's ability to unmatch and match the skis and combine these movements with a wedge turn. Encourage the match and skid movement at the completion of the turn.

Terrain and Conditions

Select moderate, nonthreatening and packed slopes for your students at this level. Practice slopes should complement the student's ability.

Mechanics

Rotary movements, edging movements, pressure control movements and balancing movements are now more interdependent and less independent of each other (they work in combination with each other). The ability to hold and pressure an edge is beginning at this stage. The students begin to utilize ski design to assist in developing turn shape. Unmatching and matching develop along with a feeling for the point at which each should occur. Two-legged steering is much improved. A feel for the relationship and mix between steering and skidding and gliding and braking is established. The use of alternating leg action while in motion is developing.

SKILLS APPLICATION

Pressure Control Movements

Encourage by shaping the turns and using maneuvers crossing the fall line.

Edging Movements

Work on turn shape and develop awareness of pressure on inside of downhill foot.

Rotary Movements

Emphasize turning both feet and turning the inside foot to match the skis.

Balancing Movements

Vary terrain to introduce more dynamic skiing.

The range of application for each skill is expanding and overlapping more with the other skills at this point. The interplay of the skills increases as the student's ability increases.

Wedge Turns with Shape

The student's ability to perform a wedge christy will be influenced by the shape of the turns he is able to do and the speed at which the turns are performed. Start out by using the gliding wedge turn and shape it. Add turns with tighter arcs, encouraging more turn uphill to finish. Put belly into the turns. Do turns over terrain that has gentle fallaway and changes in its shape. Under these conditions matching will often happen spontaneously. Introduce turns at slightly higher speeds but keep in mind the ability and comfort zone of your students.

Slipping Wedge Traverse

In a gentle wedge position with the skis pointing across the slope, encourage a high stance with increased pressure on the inside of the downhill foot. Edge engagement should be weak at this point but sufficient to support a slipping traverse. This exercise will teach edge control movements and help students over terrain that may otherwise be too much of a challenge.

Traverse to a Turn

Simply combine the slipping wedge traverse with a wedge turn. This exercise often results in a spontaneous matching. Emphasis is on the turn and its shape with the traverse as a tool to help the students get from one point to another.

Variations in Wedge Width

Have your students perform turns beginning with wide, medium and narrow wedge widths. Making adjustments in wedge width and using varying terrain will often result in very relaxed wedge christies without using contrived exercises.

For those who may still be having some problems, emphasize turning or steering the inside leg to facilitate matching. With this active matching movement, encourage a skid after the fall line.

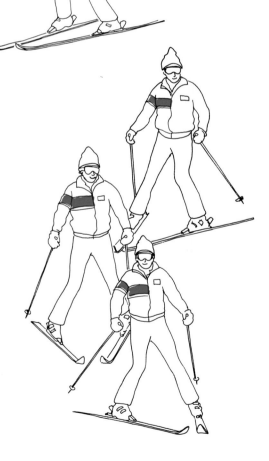

Fall Line Skid Exercises

1. Have your students start in a gliding wedge with the skis pointing into the fall line. Make very short, wiggle-like wedge turns in the fall line. Encourage the pivoting of both skis (braquage) to make the turns.

2. Work at turning both feet in the same direction out of a small wedge.

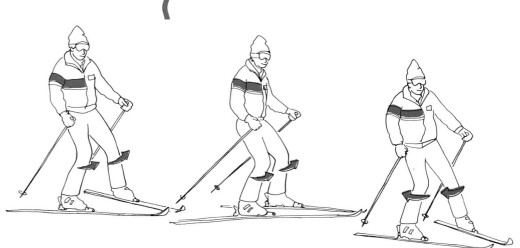

3. Make small wedge garlands across the slope in both directions. Start in a shallow line for the first garlands and then steepen as the students become more proficient with the maneuver. Continue to emphasize turning skills. Remind your students to turn both legs in the desired direction of travel. Actively turning the inside leg encourages matching and results in a christy.

4. Progress to having the students perform two wedge garlands and turn, then two in the other direction and turn, and then have them do one garland and turn. This will induce skidding spontaneously.

5. Have your student do the slipping wedge traverse, introduced earlier as an exercise, and add round turns to it. Continue to develop turning skills and encourage a soft weight transfer followed by a slight sinking to match. Sinking helps maintain balance and supports gentle edging movements.

Vary the terrain the students are skiing on and use a narrow wedge with more turning and skidding on flat terrain. Encourage the use of pressure and edging movements to control speed and direction of travel on steeper terrain.

Wedge Christy

The purpose of the exercises suggested has been to lead the student to a spontaneous wedge christy. Their first turns were characterized by tentative matching and skidding at the very end of the turn. Have your students consciously change the place where the skis are matched. Adjust the matching to coincide with terrain and speed changes. Slow turns on shallow slopes will have a later matching; faster turns on steeper slopes will be characterized by an earlier matching. The uphill christy fan started from a slipping wedge traverse is a good exercise for practicing matching and turn completions.

The wedge christy is intended to lead gently to more efficient turns. An active effort to match the skis and a positive two-footed steering guide students easily to the first open stance parallel turns. The open stance parallel turn is our next objective.

As we progress toward open stance parallel with our students, the objective is to match the skis earlier and earlier in the turn.

Open Stance Linked Parallel

Perform turns with a variety of turn shapes.

Execute turns with the skis in a parallel relationship. Emphasize the development of rotary movement skills. Link parallel turns; emphasize turning with rhythm. Begin to explore the range of edging and pressure control movements and their relationship to turn shapes. Help the student relate to the movements and feelings associated with the initiation and finish of the turn.

Terrain

Continue to ski gentle terrain. On gentle terrain the student can stay closer to the fall line, making it easier to start each turn. Your students should be able to link turns without fear of gaining too much speed.

Terrain selection is either a help or a hindrance to skiers. As skill level improves, steeper and more difficult terrain can be used to enhance growth in ability. More difficult terrain should not be introduced at the same time new movement patterns are being taught.

Mechanics

At this level, the wedge is no longer the only platform from which maneuvers are initiated. Movements that enhance skills application are now part of the student's performance pool. Turns are characterized by a slight up movement to release edge at the initiation and a flexing to increase edge angle through the turn. Rotary movements guide the skis through the turn and lead to a simple edge engagement as the turn is completed.

A subtle weight transfer is applied at this stage of skiing. Rotary movements, pressure control movements and edging movements are also becoming more refined.

SKILLS APPLICATION

Pressure Control Movements

Edging Movements

Balancing Movements

Rotary Movements

At this level of skiing the basic skills not only overlap but support one another in application. Exercise lines are used to assist students in strengthening their use of the skills. The instructor's job is to use exercises to accomplish an objective, e.g., skating to enhance pressure control movements, edging movements and balancing movements.

Open Stance Parallel

Some students spontaneously progress from a wedge christy into open stance parallel without going through buildup exercises. For such individuals the following sequence of exercises should be used to strengthen the skills they have already developed. Others need these and additional exercises to do their first parallel turns.

**Christy Fan
or
Uphill Christy**

Begin in a high stance doing a shallow slipping traverse. Sink down and turn both legs (skis) uphill and christy to a stop. Repeat this exercise several times to get the feeling of two-legged turning from a parallel position.

After success with this maneuver from a shallow traverse, move progressively nearer to the fall line with your start. Now begin at a point where you will have to cross the fall line slightly in order to finish in the same direction as in the first turns. Increase speed and seek greater change in direction. Emphasize turning both legs in the desired direction of travel.

Fall Line Open Stance

On a gentle slope start in a high stance. Make foot turns (think of turning the feet only) just crossing the fall line. Make the same shape turns but feel the involvement of the feet and knees. Make the turns rhythmical using a gentle up to start and a down to continue the christy action. Add rhythm turns with slight up and down motion.

Now smooth movements out and you have a good short radius parallel turn.

Parallel Turns with Weight Transfer

Begin either from a side track or a wedge position. From the fall line slightly flex down and turn the right ski as you pick up on (take pressure off of) the left ski and gently turn it to the left. (You will turn left.)

From the fall line, slightly flex down and turn the left ski as you pick up on the right ski and gently turn it to the right. You will turn right. (You may emphasize flexing and pressuring the outside ski of the turn. We have talked of taking pressure off the inside ski because it decreases the tendency to turn the hips in the direction of the desired turn.)

Repeat the moves already practiced, emphasizing flexing of the joints over the weighted ski, and rhythmically move from one turn to another.

LIGHT   HEAVY

right turn

HEAVY   LIGHT

left turn

Using the Poles   The pole can be introduced as early as the wedge christy, but we generally feel that it works better and is less confusing when introduced with the open stance parallel. Initially the pole touch is used to draw the skier into the turn, but remember that the pole touch gives many signals. Demonstrate simple rhythmical movements of the pole and encourage your students to incorporate pole touch in the flow of their turn. Pole touch triggers the turn, provides timing and rhythm, helps with balance and separates one turn from another.

**Open Stance
to Linked
Parallel**

In the last section, we talked about terrain as a variable linked parallel that can be used to help the student learn. Speed is also a variable that you can use to create different learning situations for the students. Begin slowly, especially in the exercises that do not cross the fall line or are not complete turns like the fan christy. To encourage a parallel relationship go just a little faster. Choose enough speed to make the turn easy without causing the skier to regress because of fear.

Have the students flex and face downhill a little more when performing the fan christy with more speed and as a more complete turn. This encourages a sound basic position through the finish of these low-phase turns. Proper flexing in the ankles and knees is important because some students will bend only in the hips and waist and end up sitting back, thus losing the ability to turn or steer the feet.

Flexing throughout the turn to aid the christy places the skiers in a situation where they must rise to start the skis into the next turn. At this stage the rising action is somewhat vertical (straight up). With increased skill and additional speed, angulation and inclination increase to offset the forces generated in the turn. We are then concerned that the "up" moves the skier in the direction of the next turn. For now, it is enough to be moving up and out or down and in enough to give the skier a rhythm and aid in the action of turning and turning with both feet.

Turns require different amounts of energy and effort. To learn open stance christies, take the skis off (on flat or very gentle terrain). While balancing against the poles, twist the feet (boots) from side to side. Use a flexing action up and down to help. Also try jumping up and turning the feet (boots) and then landing. (This energetic and athletic movement is fun but not meant for every student.)

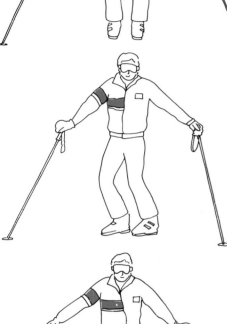

Now put the skis back on and on very gentle terrain, continue the feeling of foot turns by gently turning one way and then the other. It should feel like the slight direction changes accomplished are a result of what happens in the feet. Now with flexing in the knees and ankles, enhance rotary movements by directing the knees along with the feet. The whole leg develops turning power, but the focus is guided first to the feet and then to the knees in this exercise. These turns must be done on gentle terrain and must be practiced over and over so the students are comfortable with them.

Moving the open stance parallel skier toward more accomplished skiing can be done in several ways. You might simply refine edge and pressure control skills and start moving to longer, more controlled turns. If that works, it's great! If not, here are a few other exercises to try.

Open stance skiers are still accustomed to skiing gentle terrain in the fall line. Show the skiers how to flex down and up, getting the skis off the snow. (This is best suited to athletic students.) Work from an excessive range of motion to the minimum amount of motion needed to cause the skis to come off the snow. This may first be tried statically and then in motion with slight turns. Work toward making turns across the fall line. The students will realize the turning power that is available to them and gain confidence in their ability to turn for control at any time and still remain in a parallel stance. Rhythm and motion are effective elements that skiers can always draw from. Because we can't hop all day, however, our efforts must be to gradually tone down the unweighting to the point that skiers can maintain strong turns with rhythm without so much up and down.

Use fall line pedal turns for skiers who are just getting started and for the top skier as well. Learning to ski from ski to ski can be a real help to all of us. This exercise can be done in the wedge, but for a skier wishing to evolve with the parallel open stance, a pedal or step turn enhances the ability to remain parallel. The uphill ski is the ski that the skier stands on to start the turn, thereby making it very difficult to stem or wedge. Don't worry about a slight wedge. A slight opening of the tips and tails of the skis is very acceptable as long as it doesn't impede the turn in any way. Stay close to the fall line and the turn is easier. To turn left, pick up the left ski and turn with both knees and feet (legs); to turn right, pick up the right ski and turn both knees and feet to the right. Start slowly and gradually develop more speed, rhythm and turn completion. When you pick up the ski, pick the entire ski slightly off the snow—not the tail only or the tip only.

The three track method is used by individuals who have one good leg and two arms. This technique is adapted from the American Teaching System.

Evaluation

When you are first introduced to your student you will need to find out how severe the disability is and what kind of adaptive equipment she may need. The evaluation is intended to find the best way for the student to stand on her ski, be comfortable and maintain balance. Usually this requires both special equipment and an individualized technique.

Following are guidelines for the evaluation:

Disabilities Utilizing the Three Track Method	Adaptive Equipment
Above-the-knee amputees	One ski and two outriggers
Below-the-knee amputees (with less than 4" stump)	Same
Double amputee with above-the-knee amputation and below-the-knee with more than 4" stump	Prosthesis, one ski, two outriggers
Post polio	One ski and two outriggers
Trauma	Same
Hemipelvectomy	Same
Hip disarticulation	Same
Individuals with one arm and one leg	One ski and one outrigger

Fitting the Ski

The length of the ski is determined by the height and weight of the student. The ski should be slightly longer than if the individual were skiing on two skis, and should be lengthened according to the student's progress.

It is frequently necessary to cant the ski for a three tracker to make the ski flat.

Fitting Outriggers

There are a variety of ways of measuring and fitting outriggers for a beginner. The grip should be placed next to the hip joint when standing (flipski in the down position, clearing the surface by 1"). The cuff should be halfway between the elbow and wrist with the opening pointing outward. Adjust the brake accordingly. As the student progresses, her leg becomes the principal weight bearer and the outrigger is shortened accordingly.

Protecting the Stump

Because circulation is often poor in the stump, it should be covered with a wool stump sock and padding to protect against the cold and falls. This is of the utmost importance. If the student has problems with a cold stump, it can be moved rapidly to increase blood circulation. Make sure hemipelvectomies and hip disarticulations take extra precaution in padding the affected areas.

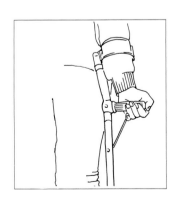

Activate the flipski by pulling up on cord. To depress flipski, pull up on cord again, press down on tail of outrigger's ski.

Walking Without Skis

Flat Terrain, Flipskis Up

Flipskis Down	Place flipskis at 45° angle to the boot. Push on the inside edge of both outriggers, hop foot forward. Use outriggers in a slight rotary motion.

Getting into Ski   Now that the student has been properly fitted, demonstrate how to get into the ski. Put all the weight on the outriggers and lift yourself up over the ski, positioning the toe of the boot in the toe of the binding, the heel in the heel of the binding, and push down.

Body Position } Correct body position has flex in the ankle, knee and hip, creating center of gravity and balance from the ball of the foot.

Learn how to walk with flipskis in the down position. Bring the flipski down to walk. Place at a 45° angle to the boot. Push on the inside edge of both outriggers and glide the ski.

When walking with the flipski up, do not rotate the arms. Push and glide as you would with the ski in the down position.

Hop Turn, Flat Terrain
At this point the hop turn is taught only as a means of changing direction while in a static position. This will assist the student in developing rhythm and balance as well as in familiarizing herself with the arm-foot coordination needed to use the outriggers. This is a confidence-building stage so pace the activity according to the individual's ability. Please note that this maneuver can be performed with the flipski in either the up or down position.

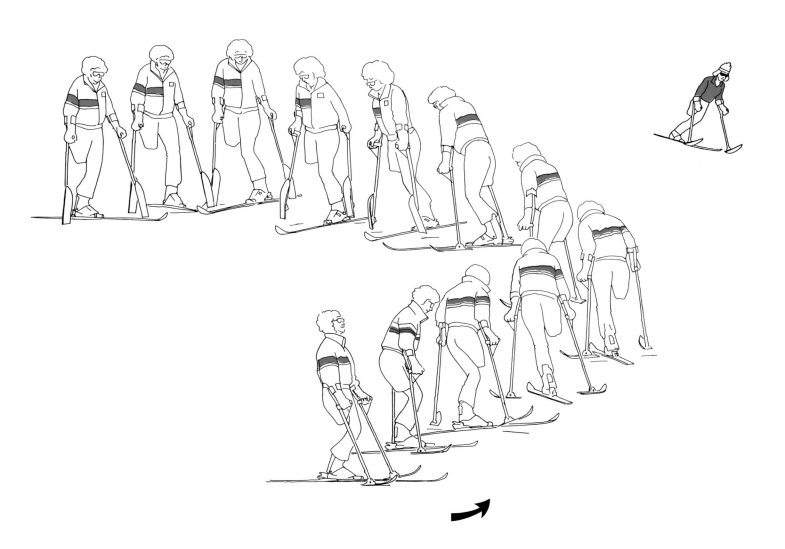

To Fall   When teaching the student to fall, show her how to lower the body holding the stump in with the outriggers up and outward, making sure the chin is tucked inward while falling in order to protect the head.

To Get Up   A beginner will find it is easier to get up when the stump is positioned uphill. Have her put the outriggers in the walking position, push against the downhill outrigger, remove the uphill outrigger and lean against it, and bring her body over the ski and push herself up.

It is very important that the stump be held tightly against the leg during all maneuvers and to protect it in a fall.

fall line

Climbing, Gentle Terrain Sidestepping is a way of climbing up terrain. What the student should learn is edge control and balance. The stump should be on the uphill side, held tightly against the body. Place the ski across the fall line. With a slight forward and uphill motion, hop the ski uphill. Stress edge control to your student. Use hop turns to get into the fall line.

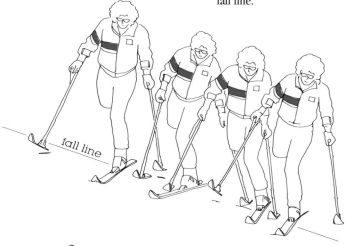

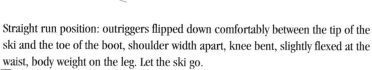

fall line

Straight Run Straight run position: outriggers flipped down comfortably between the tip of the ski and the toe of the boot, shoulder width apart, knee bent, slightly flexed at the waist, body weight on the leg. Let the ski go.

To Stop Use the outriggers as brakes, lower the elbows to the hips and push into the bottom of the outriggers.

When working on the straight run, the terrain should be gentle. It is important that most of the body weight be carried by the leg. When the student has accomplished the straight run to a stop, she is ready for the chairlift.

Loading the Chairlift

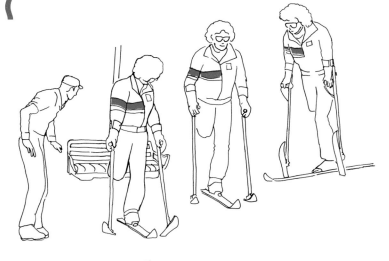

In loading the chairlift, have your student watch how other people load. Move into the loading area, flip the outriggers in the down position, look to the inside and sit down. Student must lift outriggers off the ground as she sits.

An important note to remember: When loading the chair, the flipski should be down to prevent breaking the outriggers and injury to the upper body. For safety reasons, the outrigger should never be removed while riding the chairlift.

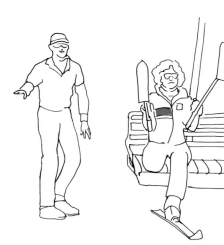

Unloading the Chairlift

As the chair approaches the unloading ramp, lift up the tip of the ski and the outriggers. Unload just as the chair reaches the unloading ramp. Lean forward at the waist, bend the knee and stand up.

Ski down the ramp by assuming the straight running position.

Traverse

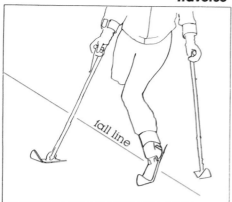

Choose gentle, wide terrain. This maneuver will require the lateral movement of the knee and ankle into the hill to maintain the edge of the ski. As the student crosses the slope, the outriggers are held shoulder width apart; the ankle, knee and upper body are slightly flexed. Use the tail of the outriggers to stop. Use hop turns to take a new direction. Repeat this maneuver several times in both directions.

Exercise: Brake and turn using outriggers to slow, leaving the ski easy to pivot in preparation for the uphill christy. For students who fear the fall line.

After the student has become familiar with the traverse maneuver, introduce steering the foot into the hill, with a slight heel displacement to help turn the ski, then releasing the pressure and flattening the ski, letting it drift toward the fall line, continuing to steer the ski into the hill as before. This creates garlands and can be used as an exercise to prepare the student for turns.

Garlands
A garland is a series of scallop-like figures carved across the fall line.

Uphill Christy
The uphill christy will get your student accustomed to the controlled skid as well as coming to a complete stop. From a traverse the skier begins the uphill christy by flexing the knee forward, followed immediately by a down motion. This releases the edges of the ski and outriggers, allowing them to slip. Steer the ski in the direction of the turn to a stop.

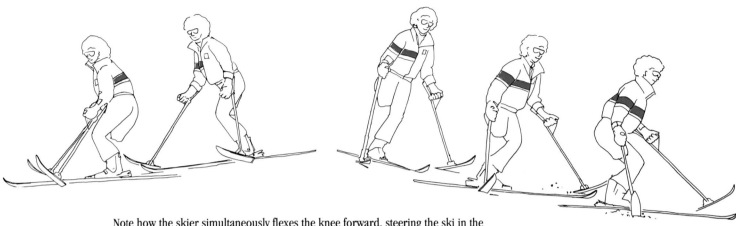

Note how the skier simultaneously flexes the knee forward, steering the ski in the direction of the turn, followed by rapid down movement. Practice this maneuver, moving to moderate terrain and on to the beginning turn.

Beginning Turns

The beginning turns for a three tracker should be performed moving slightly in and out of the fall line by using a relatively flat ski, emphasizing the steering of the foot and displacement of the heel. This will prevent overuse of the ski edge as so many beginners often do in attempting beginning turns. Avoid using the knee to steer.

As the skier progresses, she should be instructed to make the arc of the turn more pronounced. This will encourage the skidding of the ski and in turn assist in control. The student is now ready for advanced christie turns.

Boot arc exercise: Adapting exercises from ATS, try this for a three tracker: Remove the ski on flat terrain. While balancing on the outriggers, twist the foot (boot) from side to side, using a flexing action up and down to help. This will convey the concept of rotary movement.

37 TEACHING: Three Track

**Exercise:
Outrigger "Pole Touch"**

Utilizing the outrigger as a pole, touch the outrigger (flipski down) lightly on the snow, lifting the other outrigger off the snow. Complete turn and repeat. This establishes rhythm and edge control and will lead to an alternating outrigger action.

Advanced Parallel Turns

The student is also ready for more difficult terrain in order to maintain a consistent speed. The arc of the turn should become more pronounced, utilizing the edge to rebound from. This action will carry the skier smoothly from turn to turn. Perfecting this maneuver will enable the skier to move on to the short swing.

Short Swing Short swing is a series of successive short-radius parallel christies with the traverse between turns eliminated. It is the distinct edge set of each turn that makes this maneuver effective in steep terrain.

Think of the leg and ski as being a pendulum moving in rhythm. The upper body stays centered over the fall line while the leg moves side to side. This motion will perform edge change, rhythm and control. It can lead the skier into the next phase: mogul skiing.

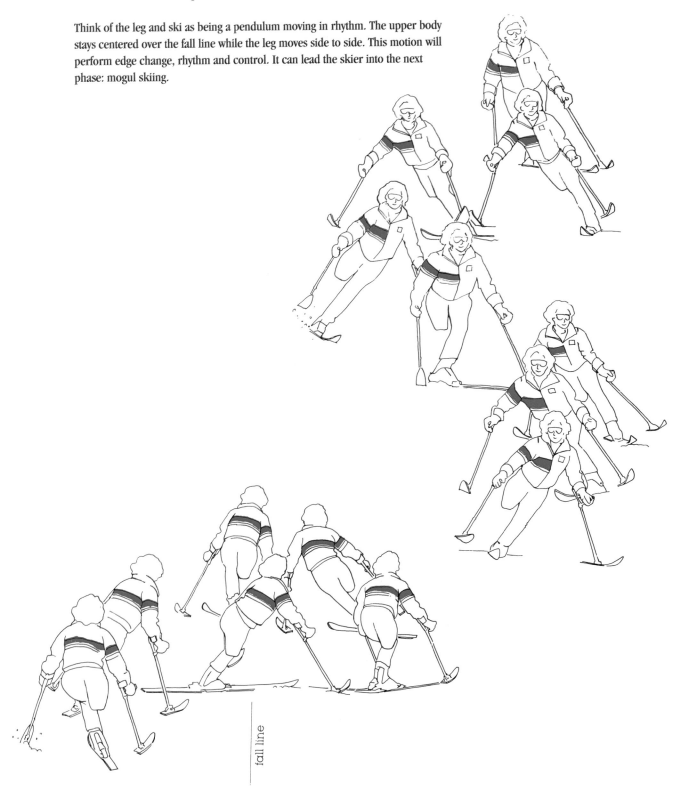

fall line

Moguls } After mastering short swing, the student is now a sufficiently advanced and competent skier to undertake mogul skiing, powder skiing and racing.

You will find that individuals who ski three track tend to advance very rapidly. However, it is important to permit the student to progress at a speed that is comfortable to her. The three track method has no limitations. Individuals with a desire to learn can excel in all areas of skiing.

Balancing skills at high speeds: tuck.

Arm Amputees

The American Teaching System applies in teaching arm amputees to ski. However, the following can assist in teaching this type of disability.

Adaptive Equipment

If the student is wearing a prosthesis, the hook should be protected in order to prevent injury and cold while skiing. A heavy leather mitten or even a cork will do.

If the student is an above-the-elbow amputee, it is advised that the prosthesis not be worn while skiing for her own safety. The stump should be protected by a stump sock or other warm material to prevent frostbite.

For the below-the-elbow amputee, it has not proven to be successful to attach a ski pole to the prosthetic side. (It should be mentioned that arm amputees on the Disabled National Team use only one pole while skiing.)

Teaching Tips

Since the amputation of an arm can cause lateral balance problems, it is of the utmost importance when working with an individual without a prosthesis that emphasis be placed on working with the feet and legs. Use simultaneous steering with the feet and legs. Frequently you will find that if this is not emphasized, rotation of the shoulders will cause balance problems.

A pole can be introduced in the very beginning to assist in walking and eventually for pole planting, to create rhythm and to help with edge change and weight shift. To compensate for the absence of an arm, it can be of great assistance if the skier imagines that the arm is still there and, through her mind, creates a pole planting maneuver on the amputated side. This will enable her to make equal arcs in either direction.

It should be left up to the individual whether or not she wears her prosthesis and uses a ski pole.

Bill Dean, former national champion and coach.   PHOTO: R.J. WALKER

Symes Amputation

A Symes amputation is an amputation of the foot at the ankle joint. This presents special problems in fitting the prosthesis into the boot with proper alignment.

Adaptive Equipment

Most individuals with a Symes amputation can be successfully taught to ski on two skis. Because of stump problems, a few ski three track. The American Teaching System applies, with a few adaptations.

Teaching Tips

Emphasis should be placed on the simultaneous steering of both feet and legs. In the beginning, if lateral control continues to be a problem, a ski bra may be used temporarily.

It is advisable that the student begin on a shorter ski and graduate to a longer ski, according to her ability.

Joe Reum, 1975   PHOTO: S. COLEMAN

}TEACHING: Amputations

Lower Limb Prosthetics

A person who has had an amputation of her leg and uses a prosthesis must have a comfortable, functional and acceptable-appearing limb replacement to enjoy activities of daily living. Routine tasks can be extremely challenging to complete when performed on one leg or on a prosthesis that causes pain with each step.

Adaptive Equipment

Those involved in teaching amputee skiing will find it helpful to understand a little of lower extremity prosthetics, especially when the student skis with the prosthesis. Just as we know that the relationship between foot-boot-binding-ski is crucial to effect efficient transmission of forces to the snow, so it is between amputation stump and prosthesis. And, just as a ski boot that is either too loose or too tight can be painful and result in blisters or affect blood circulation, an ill-fitting prosthesis can cause similar conditions and worse.

The situations that affect comfort, function and ultimately the quality of the skiing experience are extremely complex: the physical condition of the individual (overall condition and capabilities, and specific conditions relating to the amputation), available technology, the prosthetist's skill and desire to innovate and the amputee's aspirations and will.

Many single below-the-knee amputee skiers use specially designed prostheses, which would mean building the limb with approximately 15° to 21° of forward lean from the ankle with the foot set in a barefoot position. Additional suspension is gained with the attachment of a "thigh-lacer." The thigh-lacer also adds a great deal of stability in a lateral sense, preventing the leg from twisting sideways under the forces of skiing.

It is not necessary to have a "ski leg" in order to get started. A standard walking leg can be used with some simple modifications. A tight elastic sleeve pulled up over the knee and thigh will greatly stabilize stump pistoning and rotation. If the walking leg is set up for an average walking shoe, you can make a wedge of ¾" to 2" to give the proper forward lean inside the ski boot. If you do this, it will be necessary to add a flat lift under the binding of the good leg in order to keep the hips level.

Often the prosthetic limb will also have to be aligned so the knee is located in line with the hip and ankle when viewed from the front of the skier. These are the basic adjustments for a skier in a single or double below-the-knee situation.

"Jill, now 13 and an above-the-knee amputee, had never skied before her amputation. With your lessons and equipment, she is as good as the rest of us and skiing is something we can do together."

The four track method of skiing is so named because the skier is actually relying on four separate ski sources to navigate the ski slope. This method allows the skier to equalize weight on both legs by using two normal, full-sized skis. To achieve extra additional balance, the four track skier uses two outriggers. Four tracking is often used with students who have had an aneurism, or have cerebral palsy, post polio, spina bifida, arthrogryposis, muscular dystrophy, multiple sclerosis and those who suffer from a congenital defect or traumatic accident, as well as others.

The ski bra or bungee cord is often used in four track skiing.

Evaluation   Four tracking has become a popular system of skiing because it is so adaptable to a variety of disabilities. An individual who has two arms and two legs, natural or prosthetic, and is capable of standing is a candidate for the four track method. Sometimes a combination of adaptive equipment is required.

Individuals Utilizing the Four Track Method	Adaptive Equipment: Outriggers Plus
Those with lack of lateral control	Ski bra or bungee cord
Inability to walk without assistance of crutches, cane, etc.	Same
Tendency to fall forward, walk on toes or lean heavily on crutches or walker	Slant board with toe raised*
Pronounced backward lean	Slant board with heel raised (if moderately involved, heel lifts not exceeding 1" under bladder in boot)

*When toe raises are used, the outriggers should be lengthened accordingly.

The ski bra gives more control to the feet, legs and hips and helps maintain a parallel position while skiing. It consists of two metal devices that are slipped over and affixed to each ski tip. One metal piece is an eyelet and the other a hook. The ski tip with the hook is latched onto the ski with the eyelet. Although the devices are hooked together, the ski bra allows the skier flexibility of movement and a constant position of the skis, which are kept 3" to 4" apart.

Consideration of the length of the skis is very important. The length can vary dramatically according to the disability. If the student is extremely weak, a shorter ski should be considered. Students utilizing the slant board with toe lifts or heel raises frequently require longer skis in order to prevent them from overturning.

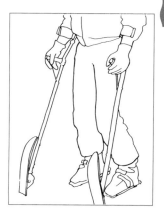

When first paired with your student, you will evaluate what her needs are and what kind of disability you are dealing with. As an instructor, your evaluation helps to pinpoint the best way for the student to stand on her skis, be comfortable and maintain her balance. In evaluating a four tracker, you will work with three positions: normal, leaning back and leaning forward. The aim of the evaluation is to create adaptive equipment to bring the individual to a balanced position. For the individual who leans forward, a slant board can be utilized to raise the toes, creating a balanced position. If the individual leans backward, then it is necessary to raise the heels. If the individual lacks lateral control of the feet and legs, some sort of a stabilizer must be used: a ski bra for the severely involved and a bungi cord for the lesser involved.

Activating Flipski (see pages 29–30 for details)

Review the equipment with your student. Explain how the outriggers work. Describe the ski by pointing out the tip, tail, edges, bindings and their use. Assist your student to find her balance and proper body position. The outriggers should be held shoulder width apart, just forward of the ski boots. They should be used only for balance with most of the weight carried by the legs. Demonstrate how to brake by lowering the elbows and applying pressure on the outriggers.

Getting into Equipment

Body Position

To establish proper body position, use the touch system in the areas of flex: hip, knee and ankle.

Moving on the Flat

Outriggers Down

Place the outriggers shoulder width apart, even with the heel of the ski boot. Turn the tips out at a 45° angle. Flex the knee. Using the inside edges of the outriggers, push off with the arms, following through with a backward thrust. Finish with the body upright in a position to repeat the maneuver.

Outriggers Up

Moving Assisted: Two Point Hold

Sidestepping

If the student does not have her ski tips stabilized and is capable of side-stepping, move to a gentle slope that has a flat outrun. This is generally not possible with students in the forward or leaning-back position.

With the student facing you, explain and demonstrate how the edge is dug in to hold against the hill. If your student is fearful, sidestep just below her. This will also allow you to help with positioning.

Falling

The four tracker learns to fall the same way as the three tracker, keeping the outriggers clear of the body. See illustration on page 32.

Getting Up:
Method 1—Assisted

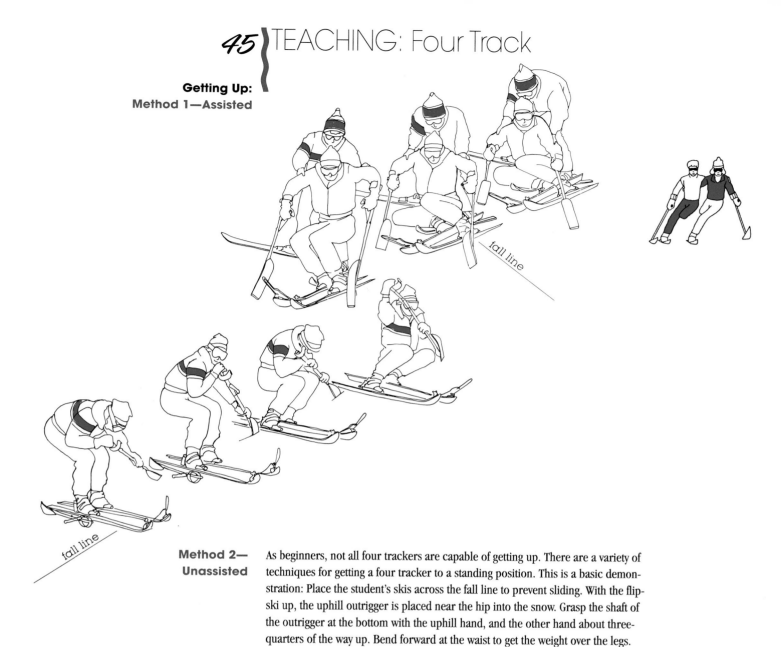

fall line

fall line

Method 2—
Unassisted

As beginners, not all four trackers are capable of getting up. There are a variety of techniques for getting a four tracker to a standing position. This is a basic demonstration: Place the student's skis across the fall line to prevent sliding. With the flip-ski up, the uphill outrigger is placed near the hip into the snow. Grasp the shaft of the outrigger at the bottom with the uphill hand, and the other hand about three-quarters of the way up. Bend forward at the waist to get the weight over the legs. Now, push up and forward until the thrust of the motion brings the body back to the upright position.

Method 3—
Unassisted

Walk the hands in a quarter circle from uphill to just over the skis while pushing upward to a standing position with body weight forward from the waist. Sometimes it is easier for the student to get up if you unhook the ski bra.

Straight Run

Gentle Terrain, Assisted

Whether a chairlift or the sidestep is used to move up the hill, the first maneuver is the straight run. In teaching the straight run you will find there is a variety of ways to stabilize the student. This varies according to the severity of the disability. The following demonstrations are two of the most common: Stabilize the student by placing one hand on the tip of the skis and the other on the downhill knee. Slowly move the student into the fall line.

Unassisted Straight Run to a Stop

When dealing with severely involved individuals, the two point hold position is utilized for additional stability. There are two ways of performing the two point hold position. The instructor places both hands on the hip or, if the student requires additional stabilization, one hand is positioned on the hip and the other hand just below the opposite knee of the student.

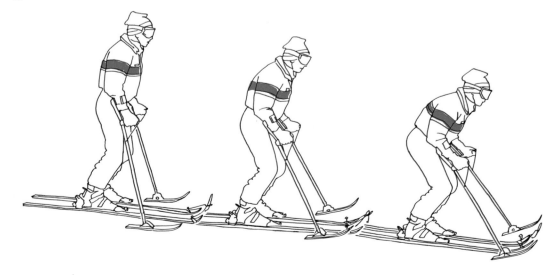

Loading Chairlift Introduce the chairlift by watching others, explaining how they load the lift. When your student has an understanding, move into the line and prepare to load. If the outriggers have a flipski, be sure it is in the down position.

Move to the loading position, have the chair slowed, and when the chair is about to make contact, give the command to sit.

While riding the chairlift, explain how to unload. As the unloading area approaches, give the signal to have the chair lift slowed. The widely accepted motion to the lift operator for slowing down is a quick downward motion with the hand, repeated as necessary. To motion to stop the chair, use a horizontal cutting motion across the neck.

Unloading Chairlift The student should hold the outriggers out in front with the flipski in the down position. When the skis make contact with the snow, have the student begin to rise up, bending forward at the waist, placing the outriggers on the snow. Ski down the ramp by assuming the straight running position. Move quickly away from the unloading zone.

Beginning Turns

Phases of a Turn
① Preparation
② Initiation
③ Controlling
④ Finishing

② ① ③ ④ ①

Determine the student's ability to find her center of gravity while moving. This will tell you if the adaptive equipment selected is correct or if further adaptation is needed.

Utilize the two point hold position by placing one hand on the hip and the other hand just below the opposite knee. The instructor should assist and encourage the student with her first turn. Make sure that the student rotates her hips in order to steer the feet and skis in the direction of the turn. Repeat this several times in both directions until the student can accomplish this maneuver without assistance, then move on to steeper terrain and beginning parallel turns. This assumes that the student is unable to steer her feet and knees. If she is able, then work first with that ability.

49 } TEACHING: Four Track

Using a relatively flat ski, emphasize the rotation of the hips and the steering of both feet and knees in the direction of the turn. The instructor skis backwards, facing the student, and with commands and hand signals directs the timing and arc of the student's turns. This maneuver should be repeated often enough for the student to become familiar with the phases of a turn.

Uphill Christy Exercise   From a traverse, have the student initiate a downward movement, steering both skis slightly into the hill to create garlands. Repeat in both directions.

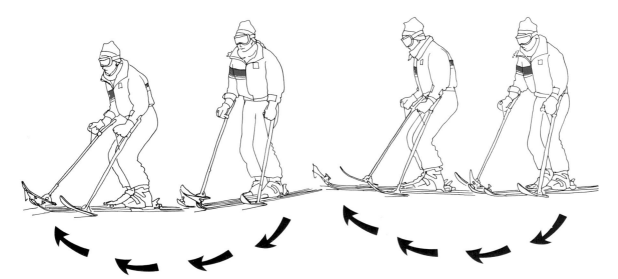

Linked Parallel Turns

As the student progresses with parallel turns, she should be taught to make her turns more pronounced. In so doing, you will find that the student will begin to slide the tails of the skis, quickly setting the edge, resulting in a rebound that will assist the skier in equalizing the arc of each turn, creating timing, rhythm and control.

In these illustrations, the student is capable of steering both her feet and her knees.

fall line

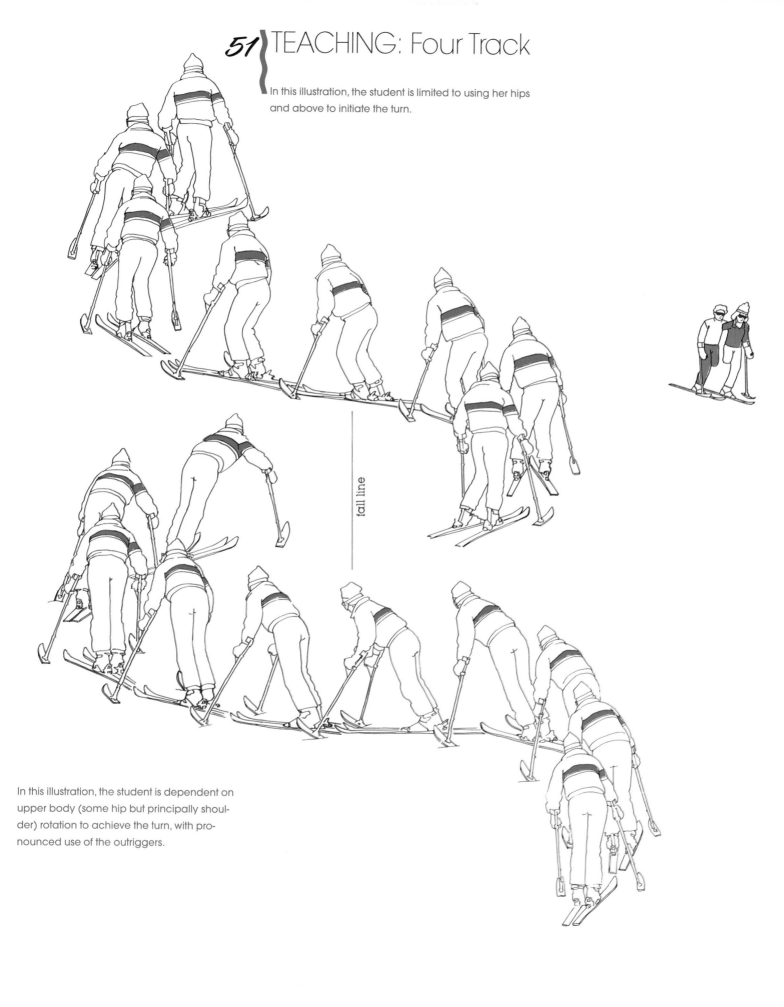

In this illustration, the student is limited to using her hips and above to initiate the turn.

fall line

In this illustration, the student is dependent on upper body (some hip but principally shoulder) rotation to achieve the turn, with pronounced use of the outriggers.

**Advanced
Parallel Turns**

fall line

Short Swing

Short swing is a series of successive short-radius parallel christies with the traverse between turns eliminated. It is the distinct edge set of each turn that makes this maneuver effective in steep terrain.

Think of the legs and skis as being a pendulum moving in rhythm. The upper body stays centered over the fall line while the legs move side to side. This motion will perfect edge change, rhythm and control. It can lead the skier into the next phase: mogul skiing.

**Moguls
Racing**

After mastering short swing, the student is now a sufficiently advanced and competent skier to undertake mogul skiing, powder skiing and racing.

Because skiers advance at different speeds, the technique could take days or months to accomplish. Remember: Skiing is not for everyone. But for those who want to learn, it enhances their freedom of movement and feeling of independence.

The reins are used primarily for speed control. However, they are also useful in assisting in beginning turns, especially for those individuals who are having difficulty initiating turns.

Reins can replace the two-point hold. (See page 46.)

The reins do not inhibit the skier's body position and can give a sense of freedom of movement. The reins are a training device and as the student gains speed control, demonstrates good turning skills, and can stop, the reins can be removed.

The reins typically are 1" to 1½" wide and made of nylon webbing. They can vary in length according to the length of ski and the size of the skier. They are equipped with a metal clip on each end.

Attaching Reins to Ski Bra
The metal snap clips of the reins are attached to the tightening device that holds the ski bra in place on the ski tips. Leverage and control may be lost if placed anywhere else on the ski bra.

The reins are positioned on either side of the skier. The instructor works from directly behind the skier. If the skier is using outriggers, reins are positioned to the inside of the outriggers.

Body Position
Eyes forward, arms slightly flexed. Center of mass is over the length of the foot. Outriggers are positioned just opposite the toe of the boot.

Bungee Cord and Pipe
When the student's legs lack lateral control and heels require stabilization, a bungee and pipe can be placed under the heel piece of the binding. The bungee and pipe should be the same width. This adaptive equipment will not only stabilize the legs but also the hips.

When placing the bungee cord and pipe under the heel of the binding, make sure they are secured tightly against the inside of the heel of the boot. This can be done by tying a knot in the bungee cord on either side of the heel. If secured properly, there will be no excessive play of bungee or pipe at the heel.

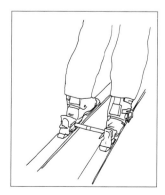

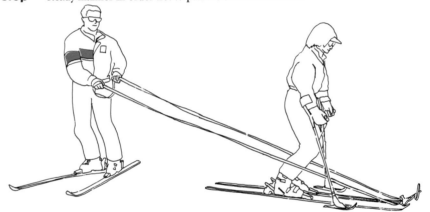

The reins can be effective in traversing the skier across the fall line.

Moving Across the Flats

Working from the front of the skier, the instructor moves the skier carefully across the flats. Care should be taken not to use jerking motions. Instead, use a continuous pulling action permitting the skier to remain in a balanced position.

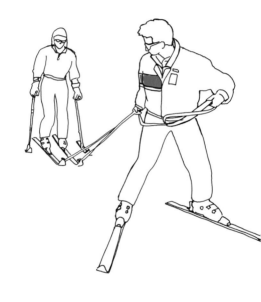

Straight Run to an Assisted Stop

During the stopping phase, tension on the reins should be applied in a continuous, steady manner in order not to pull the skier off balance.

Straight Run to an Unassisted Stop

The skier is instructed to bend elbows, applying pressure downward. This will cause the tip of the ski on the outrigger to move upward, thus activating the brake located on the tail of the outrigger ski, bringing the skier to a full stop. Beginning terrain with gentle run-out should be used.

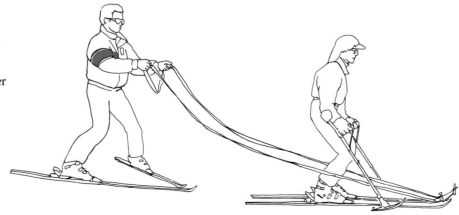

Introducing Steered Turns with Assist

From the fall line, using a flat ski, the skier steers both feet and knees in the direction of the turn. Repeat in both directions until the skier becomes familiar with the phases of the turn.

Using the Reins While Turning

If the instructor increases the tension on the reins to the inside of the turn, the skier will follow in that direction. The instructor must take care not to pull so hard on the reins that the ski tips lift off the snow.

Beginning turns are from the fall line. The skier can assist the turning phase of the turn by opening the door with the outrigger. The instructor can use the above method to create turn shapes. By moving slightly in and out of the fall line the skier will become familiar with this system, which therefore creates speed control and proper turning technique. Once the skier becomes proficient with this, the instructor may consider removing the reins.

**Exercise:
Uphill Christy to a Stop with Assist**

From the fall line the student is instructed to steer both feet in the direction of the turn. The instructor can gently pull on the inside rein to assist the skier in completing the phase of the uphill christy. Repeat in both directions.

Cerebral palsy has many different forms. This section concentrates on hemiplegia—involvement of one side. Other forms are: quadriplegia and diaplegia. The basic instruction that follows can be adapted to the individual case utilizing ATS whenever possible.

Evaluation

When introduced to your student, you will evaluate her special needs. Cerebral palsy affects the brain, causing balance and coordination problems. For a beginning skier, it is the most difficult of all disabilities to work with. Its effects can range from slight to severe impairment of mobility. During the initial evaluation you will find that no two individuals are alike. Equipment as well as technique must be modified for each person. In some cases, a combination of adaptive equipment is required.

"While her cerebral palsy prevents her from walking without assistance, you refused to allow it to prevent her from skiing."

Effects of Cerebral Palsy	Adaptive Equipment
Difference in leg length	Heel lift placed underneath bladder in boot or binding or slant board in severe cases.
Lack of lateral control	Ski bra or bungee cord
Inability to walk without assistance of crutches, cane, wheelchair, etc. attached	Outriggers (for those capable of grasping). In some instances instead of outriggers, a walker with skis or, as an alternative, a sit ski is used.
Tendency to fall forward, walk on toes or lean heavily on crutches or walker	Slant board with toe raised (degree varies according to the severity of cord restriction)
Pronounced backward lean	Slant board with heel raised
Scissor gait	Toe bar with or without heel spreader

Teaching Tip: Avoid any abrupt physical contact (e.g., a sudden slap on the back) or loud commands. A surprised reaction from the student could momentarily disorient her or even cause her to lose her balance.

Do not use ski poles in the beginning. The reason is that people with cerebral palsy have a tendency to overgrip. As the student progresses, poles can be introduced. Use a ski bra in the beginning to stabilize the tips of the skis. Doing so will stabilize the legs and hips. Depending on the severity of the student's involvement, a bungee cord may be substituted for the ski bra. A lift is used to correct a leg length difference. In most cases, 135 cm (53") skis are used for all beginners. However, it does vary according to the height, weight and ability of the individual.

If the student is unable to maintain a proper position, a slant board can be utilized to correct the position by raising the toes or heels according to the needs of the individual.

If the student's balance is marginal and she is capable of grasping outriggers, a modified Canadian crutch with a ski tip should be used.

Getting into Equipment Begin your lessons by familiarizing your student with the equipment. Explain the parts of the ski. Demonstrate how to enter and exit the bindings. Have your student try it without assistance.

In assisting a hemiplegic with getting into her equipment, start with her strong side.

Body Position Once your student is in the equipment, help her find her balance. Demonstrate the proper body position. While on flat terrain, have your student get used to her new feet by moving around a little. Watch her carefully for signs of fatigue.

To establish proper body position, use the touch system in the areas of flex: hip, knee and ankle. To keep the weak arm from flailing, teach the student to grasp the edge of the parka or to put it in her pocket.

Sidestepping During the warmup determine if your student is capable of sidestepping or whether the chair lift must be used to find a gentle slope. If your student is able to sidestep, move to a terrain that has a slight incline and a sufficiently flat outrun.

If the student has difficulty in sidestepping, place her strong side downhill. Hold her downhill hand and pull gently while pressing the back of your hand against her hip to force edging. During the sidestep explain and demonstrate how the edge is positioned to keep the ski from sliding.

Throughout your lessons, your demonstrations provide the student with visual images to imitate. You may find a slight exaggeration is necessary. When working with your student, work from the stronger side and use the touch system.

Falling and Getting Up

Explain and demonstrate the proper way to safely fall and get up. Keep the hands clear when falling.

If assistance is needed, place the student's skis across the fall line, stronger side downhill, and help the student to rock sidewise, on a count of three, to a standing position.

With some students it may be necessary to unfasten the ski bra during this maneuver. If unassisted, the student uses her strong side uphill and pushes off with the strong arm, keeping body weight forward from the waist.

Straight Run

In the beginning it is important to work toward straight running because it will reinforce better weight distribution and more symmetrical body posture. You may assist your student in this maneuver by holding the ski tips while you maintain an inverted wedge or use the two point hold.

While giving one command at a time, encourage the student to distribute weight evenly, look ahead and flex the ankles and knees forward. Repeat the straight run until the student maintains good balance and body position and becomes familiar with the equipment.

Loading the Chairlift

Introduce the chairlift by watching and explaining how others load the lift. When the student understands, move into the line and prepare to load. You may need to guide your student by holding the arm above the elbow on the stronger side and asking the attendant to slow the chair. You can use the two point hold position to move a severely involved student to the chairlift: one hand on the waist and the other on the opposite knee, moving with the student to control movement.

Move to the loading position and when the chair is about to make contact, give a clear command to sit. It may be necessary to apply pressure to the stomach to encourage the student to bend. While riding, have the student sit back in the chair. If the student is prone to seizure, use a pole placed across the lap and insert it under the arm of the chair as a safety device. Also take this opportunity to explain how to unload.

Unloading the Chairlift

As the unloading area approaches, remove the pole and check to see if all equipment is free from the chair. When the ski makes contact with the snow, have the student begin to rise up and move forward. You may wish to assist by using the two point hold position. Once off, clear the unloading area as quickly as possible.

Wedge Turns and Weight Transfers

An athetoid skier turns by stabilizing the hands as shown and dropping the shoulder, pointing elbow toward heel and steering the feet.

The hemiplegic turns by stabilizing the weak hand as shown, dropping that shoulder and then reaching downward toward the boot on the strong side and steering the feet.

Wedge Turns

For individuals who can form a wedge without increasing spasticity, begin with a tip assist. While moving, repeat over and over the turning instructions:

• Drop your elbow down to the heel of your boot,
• Come to center,
• Slide your hand to the heel of the boot,
• Come to center.

Then have your student try unassisted.

Open Stance Parallel Turns

Although some students are capable of performing the wedge, for many it will increase spasticity, so teaching open stance parallel turns is recommended. Utilize gentle terrain to introduce beginning parallel turns. Use the two point hold position for either wedge or open stance parallel.

Have the student steer both feet and knees into the hill to perform an uphill christy. The uphill christy turn should be repeated in both directions until the student is capable of turning to a stop unassisted. If the student indicates that she has sufficient lateral control, try removing the stabilizers from the tips of the skis. After your student can successfully do an uphill christy in both directions, introduce linked open stance parallel turns. Explain and demonstrate a series of turns. Point out how to ski slightly in and out of the fall line, how to utilize the christy to link your turns, how to equalize the arc of each turn in both directions and how to develop a rhythm so that the turns are fluid.

Introduction of Poles

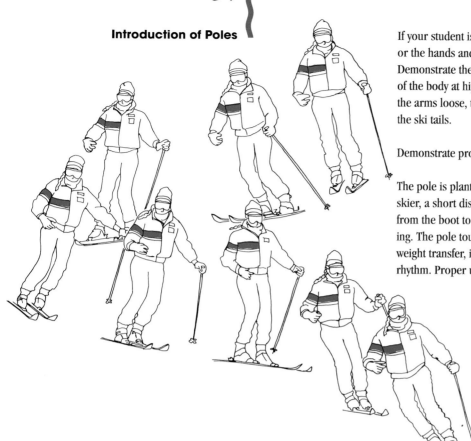

If your student is capable of controlling her hand or the hands and arms, poles can be introduced. Demonstrate the proper position: hands forward of the body at hip level, shoulder width apart with the arms loose, tips of the poles pointed toward the ski tails.

Demonstrate proper pole usage.

The pole is planted on the downhill side of the skier, a short distance away from the ski, midway from the boot to the tip of the ski prior to turning. The pole touch should be used to assist weight transfer, initiate the turn and create rhythm. Proper use takes continued practice.

See page 37 for students who use outriggers instead of poles.

Advanced Parallel Turns

Now a series of parallel turns can be linked down the fall line by using rapid weight transfer. This enables a student to maintain proper arc of the turn, rhythm and control.

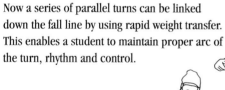

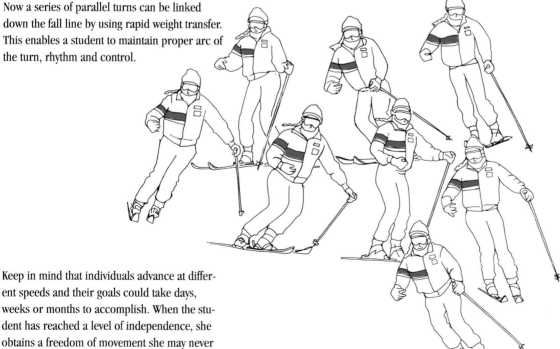

Keep in mind that individuals advance at different speeds and their goals could take days, weeks or months to accomplish. When the student has reached a level of independence, she obtains a freedom of movement she may never have experienced before.

Perhaps nowhere is ATS more readily the basis of instruction than in teaching the blind. The basic adaptation is in communicating through talk and touch to replace the function of vision. This section provides hands-on teaching tips. Essentially, all blind skiers can learn ATS and are two track skiers.

Blind people are capable of being taught to ski in a very short period of time and can become very proficient and capable of skiing moderate to difficult terrain, including moguls.

Adaptive Equipment

The degree of visual impairment can vary from legal blindness to total blindness.

Note that the blind skier can use a ski bra to establish early balance.

First Steps

Speak to the visually impaired student to make her aware of your presence. Modulate your voice, speaking clearly and looking directly at the individual. Do not raise your voice if she does not have a hearing impairment. You want to instill confidence, making sure you are communicating.

Be aware of the skier's balance and any problems she might be having with inner ear equilibrium—the source of her balance. Do not take her arm, but permit her to take yours. Be aware of barrier problems: stairs, curbs, changes in terrain, snow and ice and other obstacles. Give only one command at a time, making it short and concise.

When walking in a crowded area, have the student place her hand on your shoulder and walk behind you. Walk at the student's pace. Keep the student informed as to her location and where she is heading. Paint a picture with words. The blind understand through description.

Introduction of Ski Equipment

The introduction of ski equipment should take place indoors, prior to the actual lesson. The totally blind person relies on feel. Therefore, when introducing equipment, the blind person should be permitted to know exactly what the equipment feels like and what it does.

Let the student handle the boot. Assist her in putting on the boot, explaining proper fit and why support is necessary. She should be permitted to put on the other boot by herself.

"His check comes from a totally blind young man who has benefitted greatly from his experiences at Winter Park. He wanted to help others, as he himself has been helped."

In the beginning the blind find it difficult to walk in ski boots, as they are heavy and clumsy. Make sure the student takes your arm securely to maintain balance.

Permit the student to explore the ski, beginning with the tip, moving downward to the toe piece of the binding, and explain how the toe of the boot is inserted into the toe piece. Move to the heel piece, explaining the mechanism and how it locks the heel of the boot in place. From there move toward the tail of the ski.

If she has no questions, turn the ski over and, starting with the tip, make her aware of the sharp metal edges and caution her to be careful as she runs her hand along the edge of the ski. Explain the reason for the groove and edges.

Explain the ski pole, allowing the student to feel the grip, shaft, basket and point of the pole. Explain why the pole should not be carried in such a manner that the point might injure anyone nearby, nor should it be placed ahead of the skier while moving. Make her aware that the pole is used to assist in walking and for balance and eventually in the skiing technique.

Give the student time to gain a mental picture of the equipment. Once she has had sufficient time to inspect and understand the equipment, she is ready to put on the skis.

Putting on Skis

The skis should be cold before placing them on the snow. After the instructor has assisted the student in putting on one ski, the student is allowed to put on the other ski. If poles with straps are being used, the student should not put her hands through the straps, as they can catch on something.

Walking on the Flat

It is possible the student has never been in the position to feel a sliding motion while maintaining balance. She will need to work with this new feeling so that she can obtain a sense of balance and feeling for the texture of the snow.

Walk her in a straight line, guiding her by putting your hand on top of her pole or by skiing in front, tapping the poles for sound.

It is important at this point to allow the student to be totally independent, since independence is the first step toward secure balance.

Walking in a Circle Directed by Clicking of Instructor's Poles

After the student has successfully walked in a straight line, the instructor should guide her in the direction of a large circle, permitting the student to become more familiar with the equipment. She should slowly adjust to the weight of the skis, the approximate length of the skis and the feel of maneuvering them and maintaining balance.

The instructor should look for the spreading of tips of the skis, as this is quite common with the beginner. Instruct the student to keep her feet parallel to one another. When speaking to a beginner, always refer to the feet rather than to the skis, as it is difficult for her to relate to the skis. In commanding the student to bring her feet parallel to one another, ask her to bring her toes in. She will readily understand this command.

Body Position: Touch System

From the beginning, the student should be taught in such a manner that she is able to understand the technique and each maneuver prior to moving on to a new one. Frustration can destroy the desire to succeed if the instructions are not clear.

Use the touch system. If the student is not aware of the required flex in the ankles and knees, touch her when the commands are given. Since she has no visual assistance, technique cannot be demonstrated. To prevent frustration, good communication through touch must be established.

On flat terrain, the instructor should explain hand position, which should be forward, just below the hips. Touch the student's ankles, knees and waist, explaining the proper flex in these areas. Explain again to the student how important it is for her to keep her weight forward.

Problems that frequently occur are incorrect position of hands, lack of flex in ankles and knees and weight resting back on heels.

Proper body position is difficult for a blind student to comprehend. Therefore, it is important that the instructor literally mold her into position by means of touch and verbal command. The fall line should always be used for the teaching of straight running. This can enhance balance tremendously.

Sidestepping

Once the student has become comfortable with her skis while walking in a straight line and in circles, she is ready to climb the beginner hill.

Stand opposite the student, instructing her to place the skis across the hill. Utilizing side-stepping techniques, instruct the student to roll her knees into the hill in order to edge the skis while taking short steps, making sure the ski poles do not get in the way. At first, don't take the student more than 15 to 20 feet up the hill.

Exercise: If student has a problem, simulate climbing on stairs.

Finding the Fall Line

Once the student has reached this distance, tell her where the fall line is located. Have the student place her ski pole just forward of the tips of her skis and move the pole in a half circle from side to side to determine where the fall line is.

Straight Run

Once she is aware of the location of the fall line, instruct her to place the poles downhill in preparation for turning her skis into it. Care should be taken that the poles are at least shoulder width apart, permitting the student to bring the skis around into the fall line. The skis should be moved with short steps. If the student has difficulty, the instructor may assist by holding the tips of the skis until the student is in position.

The student should be permitted to move down the hill in a straight run. This maneuver should be repeated several times.

Falling and Getting Up

Practice, with assistance, a fall and then how to get up so the student learns the sensation and correct method.

Getting Up Unassisted

Have the student try this method or alternate method shown on page 88.

Gliding Wedge

On flat terrain, instruct the student to lift the heels of the boots outward, forming a wedge. After she understands that the wedge position is maintained by keeping the tails of the skis outward by pressure from inside the heel of the boot, she should be permitted to attempt the maneuver. Once the student is in position on the hill, have her repeat the maneuver as she was instructed. Make sure she understands that the hips should be centered between the skis, hands should be held forward and slightly below the waist, knees and ankles flexed forward. Encourage her to move down the fall line in a relaxed position.

Use touch system to assist in wedge position.

The student follows the clicking sound of instructor's poles.

Guided Practice

- The instructor selects the correct and most appropriate focus based on the student's goals, current level of skill development, attention span, ability to concentrate, etc.
- The instructor gives feedback and reinforcement that are timely, accurate and scheduled to achieve maximum effect.
- Practice is paced correctly, thereby helping the student avoid overload and frustration.

The instructor is actively involved with the student, guiding and shaping the actual skilled movement patterns the student is practicing. This can be accomplished in a variety of ways: hands-on manipulation, verbal/cognitive instructions. The amount and degree of guidance offered by the instructor can vary greatly. Many of the successes that the student experiences in learning and performing can be directly related to the quality of the instructor's guidance. However, a number of downside risks are associated with guided practice. The student can easily become too dependent on guidance during the early stages of skill acquisition due to its exceptional performance enhancement qualities. The problem with hands-on physical manipulation is that it changes the way the movements feel to the student, which makes it harder for her to retain and reproduce them. On a cognitive level, if the instructor makes decisions for the student, totally controlling the learning environment, the student never develops the knowledge and understanding necessary to independently analyze, assess and apply the skill. And, most important, to learn movements correctly, the human system must be given the chance to experience them incorrectly. Experiencing errors makes it possible for students to differentiate movements, selecting those that will create the desired performance. This experiential process is required if students are to learn how to identify, adjust and correct movements during performance.*

A bamboo pole is an aid in teaching a wedge. Illustration demonstrates a stop. Instruct the student to remain forward on the balls of the feet when stopping.

* Excerpts reprinted with permission of the Professional Ski Instructors of America from *Strategies for Teaching: American Teaching System*, P.S.I.A., Publishers Press, Salt Lake City, Utah. © 1987 and *American Teaching System: Alpine Skiing*, P.S.I.A., © 1993.

To Stop Once she has become secure with the gliding wedge, introduce a controlled wedge to a stop. At this time the instructor decides whether the student is ready for the chairlift.

Chairlift Loading Describe the chairlift and explain loading and unloading procedures.

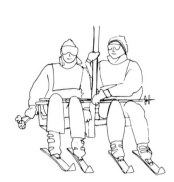

Always use the patrol or employee entrance.

Explain to the student how to hold her poles and have her take your arm as you lead her to the loading area. The blind student should load on the inside, closest to the lift attendant. Explain the chair as it approaches. Instruct your student to sit when the chair touches the back of her legs.

Unloading Chairlift When preparing to unload, keep tips up, place feet down on the snow, have the blind student take your arm, stand up and remain forward (do not wedge). Guide the student out of the unloading area.

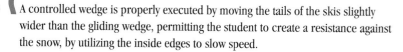

Controlled Wedge

A controlled wedge is properly executed by moving the tails of the skis slightly wider than the gliding wedge, permitting the student to create a resistance against the snow, by utilizing the inside edges to slow speed.

Frequently problems occur when the student does not understand body position. If problems occur, reinforce by tapping the inside of the boot. Hip projection from one side to the other can cause one side to be flat and the other to be rolled on edge. The instructor can correct this by skiing behind the student, placing his hands on the student's hips and centering her weight over the skis. Student practices this maneuver for some time to perfect control, body position and balance.

Linking Wedge Turns

Instruct the student to initiate a turn by steering both feet in the direction of travel while maintaining a wedge. Permit the student to link her turns in and out of the fall line. Make sure timing and rhythm are used in order to make a smooth transition from one direction to another.

Do not use "Right" or "Left." Permit the student to choose the direction. Once she has chosen the direction, use the commands "Turn" and "Go."

The blind student has difficulty in equalizing the arc of the turn in either direction. The instructor should correct this with verbal commands, instructing the student to complete each turn. The uphill christy to a stop can help the student understand the proper arc of a turn.

It is very important for a blind student to use a steered turn. She should be made aware of the fact that the turns are initiated by turning both feet and knees at the same time in the direction of travel. If she does not utilize both feet at the same time, crossing of the skis will occur.

The instructor becomes a magnet for the student through verbal commands and the clicking of poles. Move the student through turns.

Uphill Christy

From the parallel position (never in a wedge) use the connecting arm to guide the student out of the fall line into the christy, enabling her to feel the proper initiation and arc of a turn.

Beginning Parallel Turns

Beginning parallel turns utilize the same technique as in controlled wedge turns. To begin parallel turns, encourage the student to release outward pressure on both skis just after the initiation of the turn, permitting the skis to assume the open stance parallel position. Use moderate teaching terrain for this maneuver.

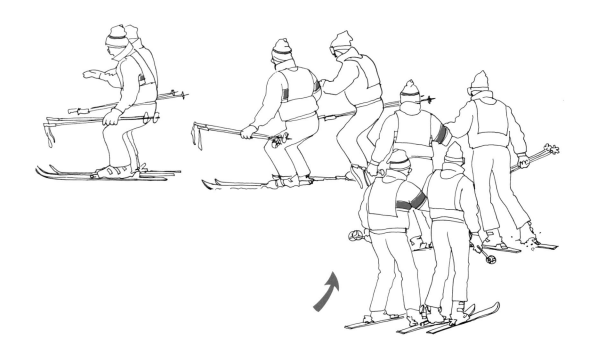

Pole Touching

After the student has successfully acquired the open stance parallel position and can turn in both directions, introduce pole touching. The right pole is planted to go to the right, the left pole is planted to go to the left. Introduce pole touching by tapping the pole of the student and talking through the motion of planting the pole. This should be done on both sides so that the student understands the technique.

The pole should be planted just forward of the feet and to the side. The pole is planted at the beginning of the turn, taking care that the student completes the turn prior to preparing for the next pole touch. Often the student will neglect to complete the arc of the turn and will initiate a pole touch in the next direction too soon, destroying rhythm and motion. This maneuver can be very difficult to grasp and has to be practiced to get the right timing.

Advanced Guiding
B3, Partially Sighted Skier

Find out how far their vision works (peripheral, etc.) Ski in front of the skier, have her indicate what range feels comfortable. For racing the range should be not more than 19–23 feet at most in front, not closer than 10 feet.

In a downhill skiing event (super G), with greater distance between gates and a longer distance between turns, the skier reacts accordingly. Ten feer at most would relate to slalom or GS events.

Have the guide wear a color that the skier finds adaptable to his sight (pink, fluorescent green or orange, etc.). If the skier can find a comfortable color, a generously sized jacket in that color that can be transferred from guide to guide if that skier changes guides.

Many skiers like verbal communication with their guide. These types of commands or controlling vocabulary will suffice for the skier: left turn, right turn, stop, go—whatever the skier is used to in commands. Use verbal commands when guiding in front: When the guide looks back at the skier, there is less chance of the skier running into anything.

When in the apex of a turn ahead of the skier, the guide calls commands at the same time he is doing the same action. When guiding in front, it is crucial that the skier and the guide work on the same rhythm and complete turns at the same time.

B2,
5 Percent Vision and Under

These skiers need a considerable amount of verbal guidance. It is up to the guide and the skier to decide on commands. The critical element is communication. Many blind skiers are comfortable without verbal commands, but from a safety standpoint, find out what the skier can and cannot do.

Ski in front and let the skier tell you what range she feels comfortable skiing behind you. It is better to be closer than to be too far away and leave the skier stranded. It is critical that the guide know where the skier is at all times and that the skier is his responsibility. No matter what other obstacles, it is the guide's responsibility to make sure the skier is safe.

The best way for the guide and the skier to become comfortable is to practice and communicate each other's needs. Nothing is more important than talking to each other and determining commands.

B1 Skiers (totally blind)

This involves complete communication between the skier and the guide. A true trusting relationship must be developed so that the skier has complete confidence in the guide and the guide can be sure the skier will follow his commands to avoid injury. It is very important that skier and guide communicate to make sure safety is their number one priority and they understand each other's thinking.

Commands for front guiding of totally blind skiers: Three separate terminologies are used: short turn, medium turn, long turn. Short turn, skier and guide need to have a concept of how long that turn will be. Medium turn (GS turn, 17 feet in length). Long turn (33 feet in length). Length of turn has nothing to do with the circumference of the turn (it means the length of time before the next command will start).

Second command: The numbers 1, 2 and 3 describe the circumference of the turn.
"1!" The circumference of an apple or orange.

"2!" The circumference of a basketball or bushel basket.

"3!" Generally a traverse across the hill, monster size turn in one direction (the length of a car perhaps).

Turn Length

Long (33+ feet)   Medium (10–23 feet)   Short (7–16 feet)

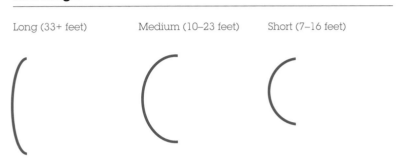

Circumference of Turns

Almost Straight
#1 Car   #2 Basketball   Traverse Across the Hill
                                                 #3 Apple

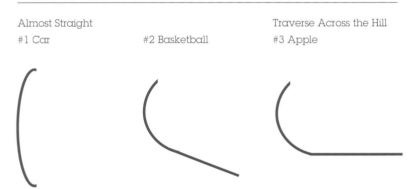

Use comparisons to give the skier a visualization in her mind about the size of the turn. A long "1" carve is used to take the skier through a long corridor at a quick pace (e.g., a lift line with few other people around), building speed. A medium "2" carve is the most common turn, a great turn for free skiing. A short "2" turn brings the skier out of harm's way. A short "1" turn is a race turn, a quick turn coming up, long term between gates. A short "3" turn will bring the skier almost to a complete stop; this turn is not used very often.

CREDIT:

DAVID PETERSON AND

GREG EVANGELATOS

Advanced Parallel Turns

Utilizing the open stance parallel position, encourage the student to increase the arc of the turn, displacing both tails to control speed. This will create a slight rebound, permitting the student to advance into the next turn without hesitation.

Emphasize control, timing and rhythm. Familiarize the student with skiing under control by utilizing carved turns, with emphasis on the completion of turns and the displacement of both tails.

As the student becomes more proficient and is skiing faster, ski as close as possible to the student. Communication is of the utmost importance at this advanced stage.

In teaching the deaf to ski, a few basic things need to be learned about deafness. The principal problem for the deaf is communication. Since they cannot hear, it is difficult for them to learn to talk. The problem is not the same for all hearing impaired; there are varying degrees of deafness. For some, hearing aids are a great help; for others, no help at all; for a few, a great annoyance. Cold weather can make a hearing aid misbehave, causing the student to lose his partial hearing. The hearing aid itself may loosen in the cold and be difficult to keep in position.

Some hearing impaired students can "read lips." The amount of the English language that appears on the lips is only approximately 30 percent. The other 70 percent is picked up from context plus a lot of guessing. Some deaf have a knack for reading lips and others never master it. Lipreading is more of an art than a science. Don't expect little kids to be skilled. You, as an instructor, must pay a great deal of attention to your student to be sure he/she is understanding you.

"It was nice to see instructors signing."

All the deaf carefully watch your face and your body language to understand what you are trying to communicate. Make sure your student can see your face clearly. Don't turn your head, don't cover your lips, be sure your face is not in shadow and keep eye contact. A full beard, a cigarette, cigar or pipe in your mouth while talking, mumbling, not moving your lips and moving your lips too much will all defeat those who can lipread.

Most of the totally deaf depend on sign language (American Sign Language—ASL) for communication. ASL is basically a foreign language. Take the time to learn at least the basic ski signs needed to teach your student to ski safely. If you go beyond this with your sign language, you will be able to chat and share ideas with your student. Wearing ski gloves rather than mittens makes signing easier. The Hotfingers cross-country gloves work well and keep hands reasonably warm.

You may come across a pupil, totally deaf, who is strictly "aural." He speaks and reads lips with varying ability but does not know sign language. You may or may not understand his speech. Some speak very well but some are unintelligible. With them, communicating can be very difficult. Speak, act, sign—anything to help get your ideas across.

Although communication is the principal problem in teaching the deaf to ski, one other problem that may surface is an inner ear problem that makes balance difficult. With some students, skiing has helped overcome the problem.

Teach the deaf student to ski by example and imitation. Indicate what you want your student to do, show him, have him do it, make necessary corrections. Always ski in front of him, backwards if necessary, so he can see what you are doing, your signing and your expression. Show or tell him what he is doing right. Instruct, but don't get too technical. Emphasize the fun of skiing, but also teach control so that he can ski safely.

Hi!

The techniques for the deaf are basically the same as for the hearing, adapted from ATS. And, we do far more than just teach kids to ski. We enhance the positive self-esteem of all our students who learn to ski while having fun.

Manual Alphabet

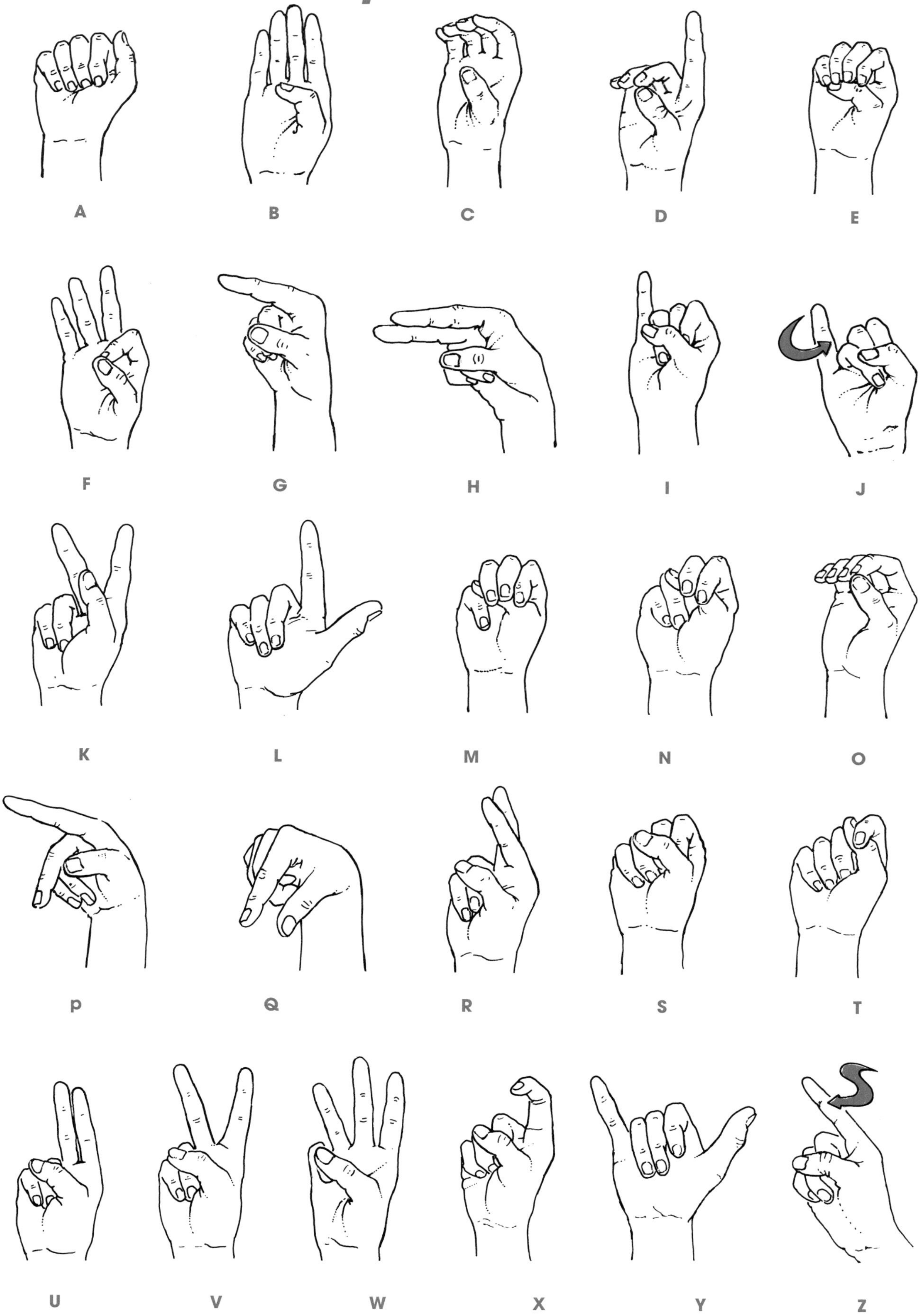

A B C D E

F G H I J

K L M N O

P Q R S T

U V W X Y Z

1   2   3   4   5

6   7   8   9   10

AGAIN
Left palm open facing right. Right hand four fingers touch left palm.

ALMOST/EASY
Both hands, palms up and fingers together. Right hand brushes tips of left fingers while moving upward.
DOESN'T MATTER— same motion up and down.

ARM

ARRIVE
Back of right open hand into left open palm.

BATHROOM/ TOILET

BEFORE
Right hand waving backwards over the shoulder.

BEGIN

BINDINGS
for skis.

BLACK (slope)
Forefinger
extended on
right hand
and pull it
to the right
across the
forehead.
Don't bend the
finger.

BLUE
(slope) Right
hand vertical
with "B" sign
and wiggle
hand back
and forth in
vertical
position.

BOOTS
Locally, use the
sign as seen in
picture except
use both hands
in the alphabet
"B" position.
SHOES—both
hands in the
"S" position.

BOSS
To let pupil
know you are
in charge, use
sign "BOSS"
plus sign for
"I" or "ME."
Cupped right
hand on right
shoulder.

CAREFUL

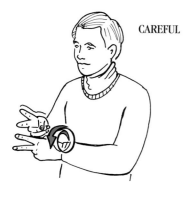

CARELESS
Sign "DON'T" CARELESS,
"RIDE LIFT" "MAYBE FALL."
DON'T FOOL AROUND on the
lift, you might fall!—"Y" hand
waving back and forth in front
of nose. CARELESS—same as
fool around but forefinger
instead of "Y" hand.

CHANGE CLOTHES
1. CHANGE – Using "A" postion
with both hands, twist together.

2. CLOTHES
Brush down the
chest several times
with the fingertips.

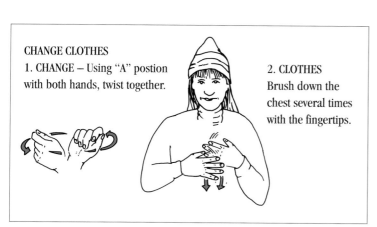

COLD
Right and ledt
fists in front
shaking back
and forth.

COME
opposite of GO
both hands/
forefingers
motion inward.

COMFORTABLE
Using curved
hands, stroke
forward first on
the back of the
left and then on
the back of the
right hand

CONTROL/"SKI" CONTROL
1. Sign "SKI" first.

2. CONTROL/ "SKI" CONTROL
Ski under control!
Look serious! Both
hands "D" shape,
palms facing in, fore-
finger out, moving out
and back alternately.

DAD
Palm flat, fingers
up. Thumb
touches forehead
for father.

DO

DON'T
Right hand in
fist, thumb
under chin.
Move thumb
forward.

DO WHAT/DO
Both hands cupped
and thumb and last
three fingers touch-
ing. Forefinger flips
out and back to
thumb a couple of
times.

DO SAME AS ME
Imitate
what I do!
"Y" hand,
little finger
to student,
thumb to
self.

DOWN or UP
Point forefinger
down—point
forefinger up.

DRINK
Lift palm up, right
hand like holding
a glass—drink.

EAT/FINISHED
1. EAT Hand to mouth—like feeding oneself.

2. FINISHED EATING Both hands, fingers extended, flip to outside. Palms up-palms down.

EQUAL/SAME

EXCELLENT

EXCUSE ME
Left hand palm up. Right fingers brush forwArd on left fingers.

FALL DOWN

FAST
"DON'T FAST"
"SLOW!"
Don't ski fast, slow down!
FAST—Both hands, forefinger out, thumb up, pull in and close fist fast.

FEEL GOOD?
Middle finger up chest then sign for GOOD.

FINE
Palm flat, fingers extended and separated. Touch chest with thumb with bumpy motion.

FINGERSPELL
Rippling (wiggle) four fingers toward other person.

FINISHED
Both hands, fingers extended, flip to outside. Palms up—palms down.

FLEX

FLEX ANKLES

FLEX KNEES

FOLLOW "FOLLOW ME" Two signs— follow and sign for I or me. Two fists with thumbs up moving in.

FOOL AROUND/ SILLY— see **CARELESS**

FUN "SKI FUN" 1. Sign "SKI" first.

2. **FUN** First two fingers stroke nose then move to back of left palm.

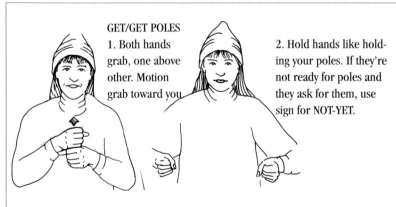

GET/GET POLES 1. Both hands grab, one above other. Motion grab toward you

2. Hold hands like holding your poles. If they're not ready for poles and they ask for them, use sign for NOT-YET.

GET UP

GLOVES Two hands alternate moving up.

GO/LET'S GO Movement both forefingers toward direction.

GOGGLES? HAVE GOG- GLES? FOG UP? SUN GLASSES? Hands held in place of goggles. FOG UP— hands, palms in, cover your eyes with hands moving around.

GOOD

GOOD MORNING Left hand out and across from chest palm down. Right hand palm up with right wrist under and touching left palm.

GREEN (slope)
Right hand with arm vertical and hand in "G" position. Wiggle.

HANDS ON LEGS HERE

HAT
Motion of pulling hat on.

HELP
Left hand palm up and lifting right fist which is facing left.

HI!
Like saluting, hand going out. Same for **GOOD BYE.**

HOT
A fast movement.

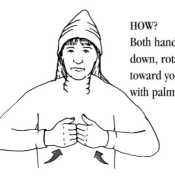

HOW?
Both hands palms down, rotate toward you and out with palms up.

HUNGRY?
"C" hand down chest. Forefinger down throat.

HURT
Both hands, forefingers pointing, twisting. Both twist in opposite directions. Done where it hurts.

INSTRUCTOR/TEACHER
Both hands held near each side of forehead with thumbs touching fingertips. Both hands move forward (taking information from your head to other person's head. Then use "person" sign, which is both hands with palm facing at head's width apart and moving down vertically.

I'LL SHOW YOU!
Left hand palm out, right forefinger point to left palm.

JACKET/COAT

LEARN
Left hand palm up, fingers together. Right hand fingers apart reaches into left hand, fingers extended—close and "brings information you've grasped" into forehead, back of hand touching forehead.

LUNCH
Right hand in "L" position touching lips.

MAYBE
Both hands, palms up, alternating up and down.

MOGUL
Both hands cupped, palms down. Walk hands down.

MOM

MORE "SKI MORE?"
1. "SKI."

2. Both hands cupped vertical toward and touching each other.

MORNING

MOUNTAIN

1   2

MOVE
Both hands in front facing down with fingers and thumb touching. Act as if you were picking up something with both hands and move them in the direction you want to move.

MUST!
Right forefinger crooked, facing down movement.

NAME
Right two fingers tap twice on left two fingers, fingers extended.

NEW
Left hand palm up, right hand palm up and fingers curved, moving down and up in the left palm.

NEXT WEEK
Left palm up, right hand moving out on left palm, pointing forward—two fingers pointing.

NO
Right hand, first two fingers and thumb closing sharply.

NOT

NOT YET!
Right hand down by side waving backward.

NOW!
Both hands, "Y" positions, facing up but moving down.

OLD
Right hand cupped on chin, moving down with fist closing. How old?

PAY ATTENTION

PLEASE
Palm of hand on upper chest. move in circular motion.

POLES
Hands at sides like holding poles.
POLES?
Pole sign plus shrug.

PRACTICE
Left hand forefinger extended. Right fist "scrubs" out and back on left forefinger.

PROGRESS
Left hand/arm extended, palm down. Right-hand palm left makes chopping motion up the left arm starting at wrist. The more progress, the higher you go.

READY
Both hands with "R" sign on each hand. Both hands with a twisting/forward motion.

RIDE-IN
(ride in lift)
Use this sign with an uphill motion to show riding on the lift.
RIDE IN A CAR

RIGHT/ CORRECT/ OKAY

ROTARY/ TURN

SAME

SAME TIME
Point to watch. Both hands fore-fingers extended touch parallel.

SAVE
To save, as a person.

SCHOOL
Left hand palm up. Right hand "claps" down on left palm twice.

SEE YOU LATER
Left hand palm facing right. Right hand thumb and forefinger extended. Thumb touches left palm and forefinger moves down a little ways.

SICK
Both hands spread with middle finger of each hand bent and pointing in. Right-hand middle finger points toward the forehead and left-hand middle finger points toward the stomach.

SIGN
If you're asking if your pupil signs, have your face looking with a ques-tion. Both hands are held (some have palms out, some with palms in) and move each hand alter-nately in a vertical circle toward you.

SIT
Right-hand two fingers once onto left-hand two fingers. Tap twice = chair.

SKI

SLOW
Right hand open, palm down moving slowly up left forearm. Fingers close (on gloves open).

SNOW
Both hands all fingers moving down. Both hands palms facing apart moving right and left. Wiggling as hands move down slowly (fast = rain).

SOCKS
Both fists with forefingers extended. Forefingers alternately brush each other facing down.

SODA POP
Left hand cupped, palm facing right. Right-hand middle finger into left fist and out and then hit left fist with flat right hand palm down.

SORRY
Right hand with fist clenched on upper chest moves in circular motion with sad look on face.

STAND
Two fingers right hand standing on left open palm. No motion.

STAY
Use sign below for THAT and point where you want your pupil to stay.

STOP!
Left hand palm up, right-hand fingers extended "chop" into left palm.

TEACH
Both hands held near each side of forehead with thumbs touching fingertips. Both hands move forward (taking information from your head to other person's head. Do this two times).

THAT
Point
with right forefinger.

THOSE
This sign as pictured
means "those" but if you
use the same hand posi-
tion and point the little
finger at the pupil and
then thumb at oneself
means "same as me."
"DO" "SAME AS ME" or
"SKI" "SAME AS ME."

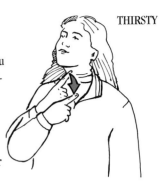

THIRSTY

TIME
Point to
wristwatch.

TIRED?
Fingertips into
armpits and sag.
Sag with shoulders
slumped.

TOILET
Letter "T," shake
hand back and
forth. Wiggle hard.

TREE

TRY/TRY AGAIN
1. TRY

2. TRY AGAIN
Both hands with
"T" position, palms
facing you, twist
outward hands
moving away.

UNDERSTAND
Right hand vertical with fist near
forehead. Flip the index finger to a
vertical position. If you question
do they understand, have your face
showing a question.

UP

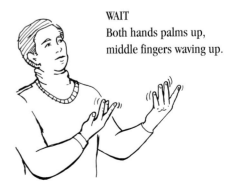

WAIT
Both hands palms up,
middle fingers waving up.

WALK
"Walk" with right and left hands, palms down.

WANT
Both hands waist level with palms up and fingers extended. Clench the fingers toward you.

WARM
Breathe on right-hand fingers.

WATCH/LOOK
The two fingers pointing forward like in the picture could be considered as "eyes" looking wherever you point them—at your skis, poles, etc.

WEIGH
Both hands with forefingers extended. Right fingers rock back and forth on left fingers.

WHAT "WRONG WHAT?"
What's the matter?
1. WHAT
shrug or right forefinger down across left palm.

2. WRONG
"Y" position up to chin.

WHERE?
Right forefinger facing up and wave back and forth.

WHY?
Right hand to right temple—pull away into a "Y" hand shape.

WIND

WINTER
Same sign as
"cold."

WONDERFUL

WRONG
"Y" position
up to chin.

YES

YOU/ME/WE
Pointing.

Four Track with Monoboard

Monoboard skiing is for individuals who do not have or cannot risk independent leg action. It is a specialized form of four track. People for whom the monoboard might be indicated include: severe hip problems; individuals with full leg braces; and individuals with high bilateral amputations utilizing their prostheses. See adaptive equipment section for description.

Monoboard (approximately 8 " wide) with two bindings.

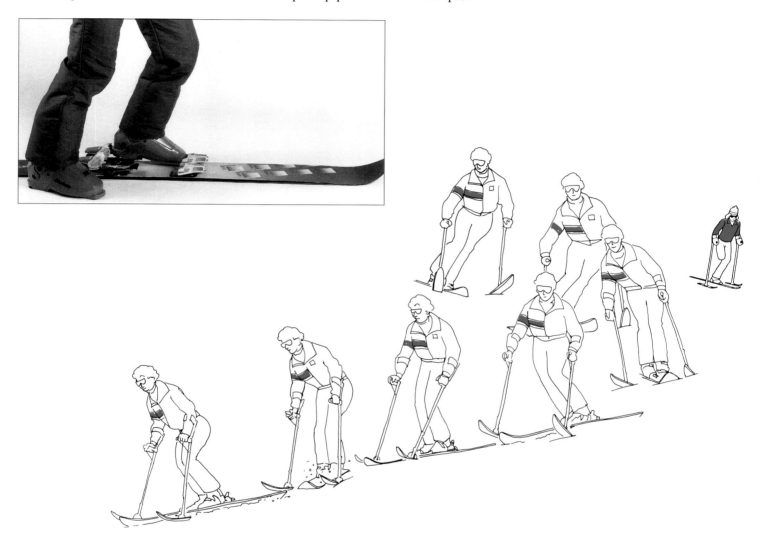

Snowboarding

Snowboarding for the able-bodied has become very popular in the last few years. For those with disablilities, it is presently in the experimental stages of adaptive development, though some individuals have successfully acquired the skill necessary to maneuver the snowboard (i.e,. three trackers utilizing outriggers). In addition, some lower spinal cord injuries have experimented with a mono ski mounted on the snowboard. At this time, precise techniques have not yet been developed; however, certainly in the near future snowboarding will become a large part of adaptive programs.

Managing the Student

In working with the developmentally disabled, you are basically using the American Teaching System. However, you aren't modifying technique as much as you are the student's behavior and your communication with them. The key is to make it fun and create a positive atmosphere.

Adaptive Equipment

Use a ski bra if the student is unable to form a wedge but only as a training device, so that the student doesn't become dependent on it.

Beginning Instruction

Beginning instruction is taught on a one-to-one basis for two reasons: The student can identify with one individual and safety can be maintained at all times.

When the instructor is introduced to the student, the instructor should have already been informed as to any type of medication, medical problems or behavioral idiosyncrasies.

Frequently behavioral problems can arise and cause great frustration for both the student and the instructor. Some of the behavioral problems can be prevented if the instructor makes it perfectly clear from the very beginning who is in charge. This will give the student a definite feeling of direction and alleviate possible manipulation.

To prevent confusion, it is necessary to be explicit in your instruction. For example, when a beginning student is instructed to sidestep up a teaching hill, a ski pole can be utilized to designate the distances she is required to climb. Objects such as a ski pole serve as visual aids in measuring distances and can prevent the frustration that may be caused by not being properly informed as to the task at hand.

The instructor should learn to modulate his voice and treat the developmentally disabled individual according to her chronological age.

The student should be permitted to interact socially. Experiences such as skiing can assist psychologically in growth and development.

"It was beautiful to watch the students improve and talk about their success. It opened some doors to inner happiness and pride—a gift that will last forever."

Do not allow the student to grasp or hang on to you. Be firm in your discipline.

Body Position

The touch system is the only way to communicate proper body position to a developmentally disabled student: hands on thighs, flex in ankles, knees and hips, raise chin to look ahead.

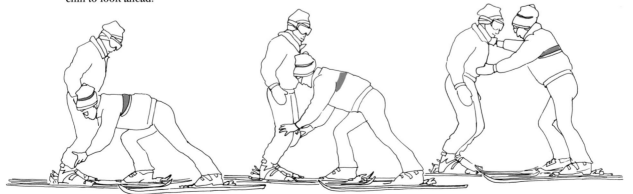

Walking

Walking the student on the flat will disclose perceptual problems.

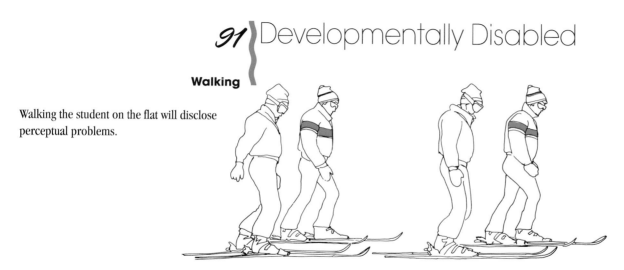

Sidestepping Stand opposite the student, instructing her to place the skis across the hill. Utilizing sidestepping techniques, instruct the student to roll her knees into the hill in order to edge the skis while taking short steps, making sure the ski poles do not get in the way.

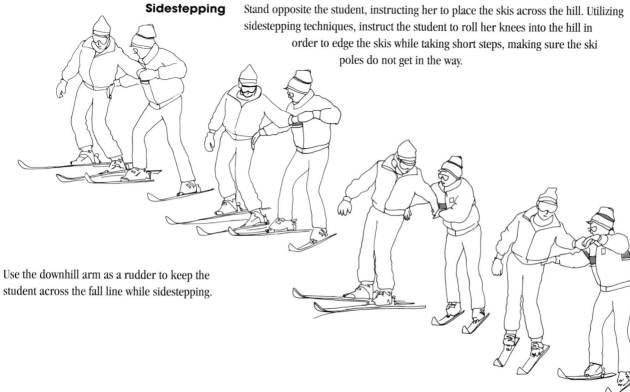

Use the downhill arm as a rudder to keep the student across the fall line while sidestepping.

Straight Run Reinforce body position for straight run, using assist.

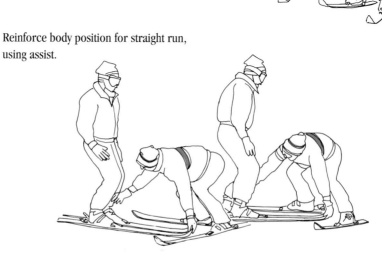

Hands on thighs in unassisted straight run.

To Fall | Teach the student
to fall on her uphill hip.

To Get Up | With skis across fall line and hands
uphill just forward of the feet, walk hands
down the hill and push upward to a standing position.

An alternative way of getting up is to have the student lie up the fall line, position
feet in an inverted wedge, pushing up off the snow, chest first, then hips.

Wedge | To prevent student from sliding backward, assist her out
of the fall line. This maneuver could also be utilized to assist the
student into the fall line to begin a turn.

The instructor signals a wider wedge and taps the pressure points.

Further frustrations can be prevented if the instructor works from in front of the student. The instructor will be in a better position visually to demonstrate various ski positions and techniques. In addition to learning from the visual demonstrations, the student gains a sense of security with the instructor ahead of her and nearby. This also enhances safety.

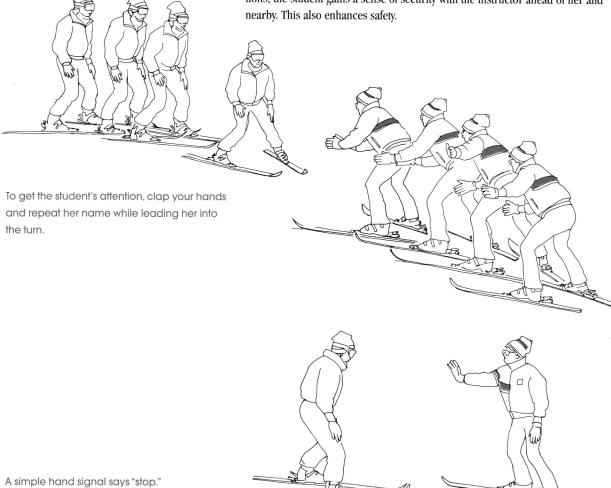

To get the student's attention, clap your hands and repeat her name while leading her into the turn.

A simple hand signal says "stop."

Sit skiing permits individuals with severe disabilities previously unable to ski to experience the thrill of speed and motion. Sit skiing was introduced in the 1980 Winter Park teaching program and became an immediate success. Over 440 lessons were provided the first season on a trial basis to paraplegics, incomplete quadriplegics and many other persons. The sit ski is a sled-like device that is controlled by the upper body and short, handheld poles. Safety of the sit skier and other skiers is ensured at all times by "tethering," in which an able-bodied skier skis behind the sled holding an attached rope.

"Your sled program is the most exciting thing I've done in the 10 years of being a quad."

Evaluation

Sit skiing can be a tremendous joy for those dependent on a wheelchair. While on the ski slopes these individuals experience a fluidity of motion in a barrier-free environment once thought unobtainable.

Adaptive Equipment

When first introduced to your student, you and a qualified staff person will evaluate her special needs. Is she a para or low-injury quad? Does she require a wheelchair for mobility? What is her overall health and physical condition?

During the evaluation you have found out how well the student can grasp. This will determine what kind of poles the student will use. The most common are the spike and kayak types. While in the equipment room, take the opportunity to explain some of the sit ski's features to the student, such as the roll bar, main shell and edges.

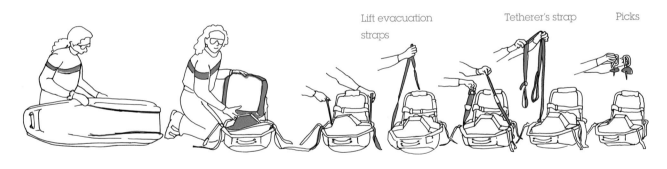

Shell and edges   Padding   Leg straps   Harness   Lift evacuation straps   Tetherer's strap   Picks

Clothing

While in the sit ski, snow has a tendency to fly up into the face of the skier, so proper clothing is an important factor. Goggles, a hat and a waterproof jacket should be worn.

Special care should be taken with quads and paras. Since they have little or no feeling in their lower body, frostbite can easily set in. Use insulated boots to protect the feet from frostbite. Layered clothing should also be worn so the body temperature can be adjusted depending on the amount of physical activity. Waterproof mittens or gloves are a must.

Getting into the Sit Ski

The student should be made comfortable in the sit ski. It is very important that the knees be slightly bent and the knee pad placed under the knees. This is to prevent hyperextension.

Check that the two front yellow straps are laid up alongside of the sit ski for easy access in case of a chair evacuation. Finally, check for any loose lines hanging out of the sled. At this point the student is ready for the chairlift.

Lift from wheelchair into sit ski.

Attaching straps.

Snow skirt over the head.

Loading Chairlift

To help ease the student's apprehension, explain how the sit ski has been designed to be compatible with the chair. Have the lift operator slow the chair. Then have the student push herself up to the chair if at all possible. While loading, grasp the roll bar on the side with one hand and with the other hand grasp the front side of the sit ski. When the sit ski is in position, fasten the safety strap and instruct the student not to lean forward.

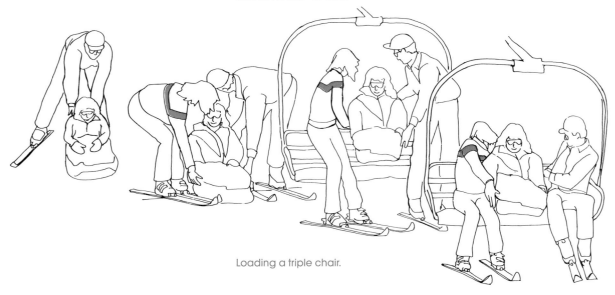

Loading a triple chair.

**Loading a
Double Chairlift**

Looking for approaching chair.   Positioning sit ski.   Attaching safety strap.

**Unloading
Chairlift**

When approaching the unloading area, signal the chairlift operator to slow the lift. Release the safety strap. Utilizing the same hand position as when loading, tilt forward and push off as soon as the front of the sit ski makes contact with the snow. Guide the sit ski with the roll bar away from the unloading area.

**Emergency Lift
Evacuation**

If the chairlift breaks down, it will be necessary to evacuate the sit ski. For this reason the chairlift harness should be easily accessible while riding the lift. Lower the snow skirt and remove the two front yellow straps. Pull out the third strap from behind the student. Attach them to the carabiner. The assembly is then attached to the safety patrol rope. Release the safety strap. As the patrol begins to lift the sit ski out, guide it sideways away from the chair until it clears and is lowered.

How to Fall and Roll

For a sit skier, a fall means the rolling of the sit ski. The roll should be practiced on gentle terrain at first. Instruct your student never to try to stop a roll. It is very easy for an arm to get caught underneath. This maneuver should not be taught to students who have recently had a back fusion.

Tetherer

Explain to your student the purpose of the tetherer, how it serves as a safety mechanism in case the sit ski gets out of control. Explain the fall line. Also explain how the uphill or inside edges are used to carve a turn.

Tethered Stop Because the sit ski's response is greatly altered in different snow conditions, pay close attention to the condition of the hill. The sit ski works best in soft-packed snow or just after a snowfall. Extra caution should be taken on hard-packed snow or icy conditions. From the beginning the student should be aware that the sit ski will not turn as sharply or stop as fast as a pair of skis. This needs to be stressed, especially to those students who skied normally before their injury. Emphasize to the student that caution should be taken when skiing through a congested area.

Emergency signal to stop.

Straight Run On moderate terrain, introduce the straight run. This will help the student "feel" the equipment and find balance while moving.

To Stop When turning to a stop, have the student ski down the fall line. The pole is then planted on the uphill side as the student leans into the hill. Practice this maneuver in both directions. If the student has difficulty in stopping, the tetherer will bring the sit ski under control by utilizing a hockey stop position.

Pole Touch The pole touch initiates the turn. Work on rhythm and upper body weight shift with your student to help understand how to work the sit ski's edges in carving a turn.

Beginning Turns

When teaching beginning turns, stress the need for smooth arc turns. Have the student start setting the next turn just before the sit ski enters the fall line.

Linked Advanced Turns

When working with the linked turns, it is important for the tetherer to develop anticipation skills. Anticipate when the student will turn and turn with her. Otherwise, you may get whiplashed to another position and be unable to help the student.

Work toward tighter turns on intermediate terrain. At some point suggest to your student the idea of having one of her friends become a certified tetherer. This will give the sit skier and her friend the freedom to ski at their leisure.

Since teamwork is very important in the moguls, explain the difficulty a tetherer has when following the sit skier. For instance, the sit skier should go around moguls, not over them. Excessive speed in rough terrain can also cause problems for the tetherer in case an emergency stop is required.

Sit skiing gives the individual who normally utilizes a wheelchair the opportunity to become an active participant in the sport of skiing, but safety must be stressed at all times.

The bi ski is gradually replacing traditional sit skis and can accommodate a wide variety of individuals with severe disabilites. The first bi ski was designed by Mike Miltner; however, some new designs are now on the market. (See page 180.)

Evaluation

If an individual is having difficulty skiing in a mono ski, or has previously skied in a sit ski, the bi ski can accommodate him in a very dynamic manner. The following disabilities are candidates for the bi ski:

1. High-level paraplegics from about T7 and up
2. Quadriplegics
3. Other individuals who use a wheelchair or ambulate with difficulty using crutches, canes or walkers; have multiple amputations; those who have traumatic head injuries and others who have not been successful in stand-up skiing.

With a complete evaluation of the skier's disability, the skier and instructor can have a very positive beginning and a quality experience.

It is the responsibility of the evaluator to determine if handheld outriggers or fixed outriggers should be used by the skier. In most cases the skier with limitations in the lower regions is capable of using the handheld outriggers. However, those individuals with higher involvement who lack the arm strength for returning to a neutral position while using handheld outriggers are usually equipped with fixed outriggers. When working with fixed outriggers, start with the outriggers farther out and move close to the unit as the skier progresses. If fixed outriggers are used, in most cases the bi ski must be tethered. However, with some of the more recent models, this is not the case. Refer to the owner's manual for tether information.

Obtain the following information in order to better evaluate the student:
• Special considerations specific to the disability
• Medications and side effects
• How recent is the injury
• Is there any additional disability that is not apparent
• Test arms for strength
• Do arms have the strength to return trunk to neutral position using side-to-side movements
• Other activities in which the individual is involved
• Trunk balance
• Arm and grip strength
• Balance exercise: neutral side to side (in wheelchair)

Chair Transfer with Assist

Transferring skier from wheelchair to bi ski.

Instructions to Verify Proper Location of the Ski Under the Bi Ski or Mono Ski

1. Mark the Ski: Measure the straight line distance from the tip of the ski to the tail and divide this distance in half. Measure this distance from the tail of the ski forward. Place a permanent mark at mid-cord position on the ski using tape or a permanent marker.

2. Find Balance Point: While in the mono ski, place a wooden dowel underneath the ski at the mid-cord. With the dowel in this position the skier should be able to lean forward and the front of the ski should touch the ground. If the seat is appropriately positioned, leaning back should cause the rear of the ski to drop to the ground.

3. Adjust Balance Point: If the balance point does not correspond to the mid-cord position of the ski, it will be necessary to move the seat forward or backward. Once you find the best position for the seat, place a permanent mark on the mono ski frame that corresponds with the mid-cord position of the ski. Adaptive ski programs with mono skis may wish to place permanent marks on the mono ski frame at 1" intervals. By numbering or lettering those marks, individuals using the equipment will learn which number or letter they will want to correspond with the mid-cord position of any particular ski. This can save a lot of time and eliminates the need to conduct the balance test each time the skier uses the equipment. Having the balance point at the mid-cord position of the ski is a good place to start. With experience you may find that your personal preference dictates that you want your balance point to be slightly in front of or behind the mid-cord position of the ski.

Fitting the Skier into the Bucket

The bucket of the bi ski should fit the skier in the same manner as a ski boot. All straps should be properly adjusted, making sure that circulation is not impaired. An upper chest strap should be used if student lacks upper trunk balance.

Fitting the Skier into the Bi Ski

The skier must be dressed for cold temperatures, especially in the lower extremities. The fitting of the skier into the bi ski is very important. An improper fit can interfere with the skier's progress and can be very frustrating.

The following steps can be helpful:

1. The cushion should be positioned comfortably into the seated area of the bi ski. Proper placement of the cushion can assist the skier in maintaining body mass over center point. If the student is smaller than the bucket, make sure to have plenty of padding on each side of the hips and back to keep the skier from sliding to one side of the seat, thus making the bi ski turn only one way.
2. All straps and buckles are placed well away from the seated area. Remove objects from the back pockets of the skier. This precaution can prevent pressure sores or possible skin abrasions. Adjust seat or footrest to give student the best support.
3. All straps and buckles should be firmly secured without cutting off circulation.
4. Easy access to chairlift evacuation strap.
5. An upper chest strap should be used if the student lacks upper trunk balance.
6. When working with a student with poor grip strength it may be necessary to Velcro hands to outriggers or T-bar.
7. It is a good idea for the skier to wear a helmet (mandatory for TBI).

Body Position and Balance

Define center of balance concept, based on trunk position and arm placement.

Moving on the Flat, Assisted

The instructor, with or without skis, holds firmly onto the bi ski and pushes the student along.

Walk forward and back. Good exercise for balancing to coordinate outriggers while moving on flat.

Falling

Raise outriggers upward and out of the way of the bi ski.

Getting Up, Unassisted

To get up unassisted, have the student position the bi ski across the fall line, with body uphill. Place outriggers uphill and push up with edge of tail of outrigger ski and rebalance. If necessary, the instructor can assist from behind.

Balance Drills

1. Practice with outriggers how to stay up, relaxing arms and keeping elbows unlocked. With outriggers on ground, slowly transfer body weight from side to side, going a little farther each time. This will also test skier's arm strength and ability to use handheld outriggers.

2. Bend upper body forward and back.
3. Twist upper body right and left.

4. Swing arms forward and back together and in position

Getting Up, Assisted The instructor removes his skis and places the bi ski across the fall line. Take hold of bucket, place foot below ski and pull upward to an upright position. Avoid pressing down on bi ski as this can cause damage to bi ski.

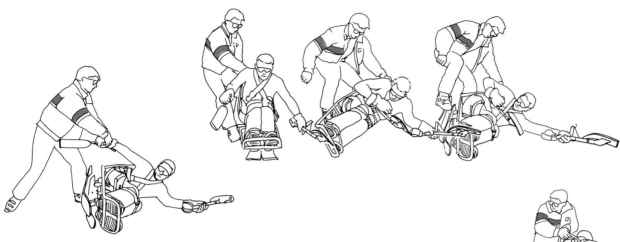

Do not assist this way. Could cause an injury.

Loading the Chairlift Instructor moves bi ski forward for loading. The back of the bi ski should align with the "Stand Here."

The bi ski is elevated, making it compatible with the chairlift for loading.

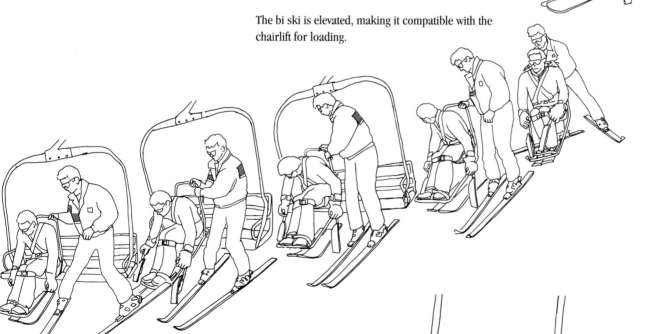

The instructor and skier sit in chair, making sure that bi ski is placed well back on chair.

The safety line and carabiner is immediately fastened to chairlift. The safety line remains fastened until skier is over the unloading ramp.

Unloading the Chairlift

DO NOT remove the safety strap/carabiner until the bi ski is over the unloading ramp. Ask for a slowdown or a stop.

Note: Some models have release mechanisms that must be activated before and after unloading.

The instructors can move the bi ski from side to side. This motion should be done as a "wiggle" back and forth, gently but firmly. The instructor should always have a firm grasp on the mono so that they will not unload too early. Make sure the bi ski points straight down the unload ramp and that the unload is as gentle as possible.

As the skier unloads from the chair, there will be a bounce as the bi ski drops onto the spring/ski. The instructor moves the bi ski off the ramp. The skier places the outriggers over his lap.

Move the skier away from the unloading ramp.

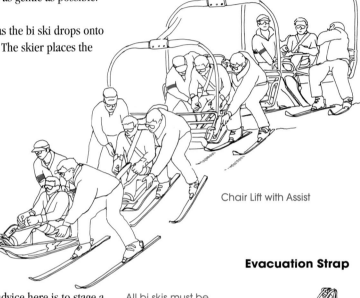

Chair Lift with Assist

Evacuation Strap

Chairlift Evacuation

Each ski area has its own evacuation procedures. The best advice here is to stage a mock evacuation with the ski patrol at least once a season, preferably at the beginning of each season. The bi ski and the skier should always be equipped with an evacuation harness that is properly adjusted and secured.

All bi skis must be equipped with an evacuation strap.

Emergency Stop with Assist (Handheld Outriggers)

While the skier moves down the fall line, instructor has the skier signal for an emergency stop by raising the outriggers and yelling "stop." The instructor goes from a wedge position to a parallel hockey stop. With the instructor's skis across the fall line, engaging uphill edges, the tether line is pulled taut. Create as many angles in the tether line as possible. This maneuver will cause the bi ski to come to a complete stop.

Fixed outriggers are used for those individuals who are severely involved.

Note: Most bi skis have the fixed outriggers mounted on front of the unit rather than the back. However, the stabilization is similar. For bi skis with fixed outriggers mounted in front of unit, the manufacturer states that the bi ski must be tethered at all times.

**Body Position
and Straight Run
(Handheld Outriggers)**

Define center of balance concept based on trunk position, arm and outrigger placement. Practice balance with outriggers next to heel of boot. Relax hands and arms, elbows unlocked, slightly flexed, next to hips. Look shoulders and eyes forward.

From the fall line using proper body position, have skier ski down fall line. Straight run can play an important role in introducing the skier to proper outrigger placement, balance and pressure.

Terrain: Begin with a good run-out.

Note: Straight run only works when skier is using handheld outriggers. If you are using fixed outriggers, the unit only wants to turn. Go from balance to uphill turn to a stop.

**Uphill Turn to a Stop
(with Handheld Outriggers)**

From a neutral position the skier moves down the fall line, turns head and eyes in the direction of travel, drops shoulder and hip if possible to the inside of the turn and continues this maneuver until bi ski comes to a complete stop.

Beginning Linked Turns with Total Assist Using Fixed Outriggers Mounted on Rear of Bi Ski with Double Tether

For the skier with fixed outriggers it can be difficult to find a balanced neutral position, because the skier has no contact to the snow with his arms.

From the fall line the skier uses rotary motion of the head and shoulder, hands and arms, dropping shoulder to the inside of the turn. Repeat this maneuver in both directions, making sure that the ski moves slightly in and out of the fall line while working on turn shape, balance and realignment, making it possible for the skier to cross over the new turn. At this time eliminate rotary when working with a bi ski that has fixed outriggers mounted on the front.

Once the skier is fluid in demonstrating these skills, the instructor can introduce more inclination, edging, rotary and turn shape, taking the skier to a higher level of skills.

Fixed Outriggers

When working with fixed outriggers, the snow conditions play a very big part in the lesson. The best conditions are when the snow is soft enough so the skis can perform well, yet firm enough to support the fixed outriggers. When the snow is too soft or slushy, the fixed outriggers tend to sink in the snow, and if this happens when the skier has much speed, it can make the bi ski cartwheel.

**Linked Turns with Handheld
Outriggers, Tether Line
(Beginning Terrain)**

Have the skier try unassisted turns while making shallow linked turns into the fall line. Skier uses inclination to turn. Outriggers are held forward for balance. Once the skier can demonstrate good turning skills by using inclination, instruct the skier to turn the head and shoulders, hitchhiking the thumb of the inside outrigger, creating rotary motion. This will develop better edging, turn shape and rotary skills, permitting the skier to move on to upper-level beginner/intermediate terrain. At this stage the skis will start to skid. In order to prevent overturning, introduce counter rotary movements to control the turn and help prevent overskidding. If the skier should overturn and the skis are pointing up the hill, instruct the skier to lean into the turn. The skis will back up in the reverse arc that he skied into and once the skis come across the fall line, the skier can neutralize and initiate a new turn down the hill.

Another reason for not being able to successfully carve each turn is that the skier's hips move with the bucket. Make sure during evaluation that proper padding is utilized in fitting the student into the bucket of the bi ski.

Quite often a more involved high-level injured will have a tendency to favor one turn direction, skidding one turn and carving in the other direction. To help correct this situation have the student push off the inside outrigger. This will assist in bringing the skier's center of mass to a neutral position, permitting a crossover into a new turn.

Responsibility of the Tetherer

When using fixed outriggers the double tether line can be more effective than the single line when teaching the bi skier to turn. The tetherer should be standing behind the bi ski and slightly to the inside of the turn.

As the outside line is raised upward and pulled taut, the inside line is pulled across the midsection of the tetherer. This will help assist the skier with weight transfer from one side to the other, creating turn shape, edge change and better control. Also, it can assist in stabilizing the bi ski by keeping body mass over center of balance.

Note: When working with a student using fixed outriggers who needs assistance by a double tether, the skier and the tetherer must work together for timing when to initiate the next turn, etc. It works very well for the tetherer to call the turns (just like working with a blind skier). As the skier (and the tetherer) progress on to more advanced terrain it becomes necessary to move the fixed outriggers in closer to the bi ski to allow for shorter-radius turns.

Exercises:

Uphill Turn to a Stop with Assist (with Fixed Outriggers), Beginning Terrain: From the fall line the student is instructed to drop inside shoulder and hip in the direction of the turn. Instructor can gently pull on inside tether line and upward on the outside tether to assist skier in completing turn to a stop. Repeat in both directions.

Linked Turns: Same as above, but after crossing the fall line, the skier drops the other shoulder and hip and initiates the turn in the other direction.

Full Bucket Assist

When working with a student, sometimes it becomes necessary to do a full bucket assist to get a student down off the mountain or over some terrain that he is not ready to ski yet. This can be a very dangerous operation if not performed properly.

First, remove the outriggers. The tetherer comes forward and grabs the handles on each side of the seat (the tetherer should still have the tether line attached to himself and the bi ski, just in case). The tetherer must ski in a very wide wedge and be careful that his skis do not cross with the tips of the bi ski. If the tetherer's ski tips become tangled with the tips of the bi ski, he will lose total control of the bi ski.

When steering the bi ski in a full bucket assist, don't try to force the bi ski to make the turn. Talk with the skier while doing this and have the skier assist you.

**Bucket Assist
Turn Methods**

1. Pressure bucket to engage edge driven turns.
2. Keep skis totally flat; instructor pulls bucket to skid skis through turn.

Unassisted practice is possible
due to the stability of the bi ski.

The mono ski is now replacing the Arroya sit ski as the equipment of the future for most paraplegics. The mono ski allows paraplegics to actually ski in a three track fashion. Designed in Germany, the mono ski was made available in the United States in the fall of 1985. Previously used only in a few European countries, it was designed strictly for the T-bar, not chairlifts. To enable the Germans to market the mono ski in the United States, certain modifications were made to their mono ski.

Student Evaluation

If the individual is athletic and in excellent shape, it is possible for an injury level as high as T4 to use the mono ski. However, a higher level of injury may lack necessary balance and strength. (See "Spinal cord injury" on page 152.)

The mono ski was designed for double amputees and low-level spinal cord injuries, although it has been successful for other disabilities. Some levels of injury are more successful than others.

If you are not sure if someone is a good candidate for the mono ski, some tests you can try to get a better idea are:

• Handshake: This will give you a good idea of the grip strength.

• Put the skier's hands on the wheels of the chair and lift body off the seat. This will show arm strength and whether one arm is weaker than the other.

• Have the skier sit forward in chair with back away from the back of the chair and hands away from the wheels and have him lean side to side and front to back. This will show the amount of trunk balance the student has.

The above tests should give you an idea as to whether the student is a good candidate for the mono ski or would be better in a bi ski. Other tests you can do after the skier is in the mono ski are:

• With outriggers on the ground, transfer weight from side to side, going a little farther each time. This will test whether the student has enough hand and arm strength to keep upright.

• Have the student sit in a relaxed position and slowly lift both outriggers off the ground and see how long balance can be maintained. When the skier is sitting balanced, look to see that the ski is flat on the ground and not up on one edge. If up on one edge, turns will be more difficult.

If the skier tips in one direction the center of mass is probably off-center and may need to be refitted to readjust weight.

Adaptive Equipment

With injury levels above T10, a higher seat belt may be desirable, not only for support but to give the skier more ability to lean forward and sideways and transfer weight for the initiation of the turn. The skier should fit as snugly as possible into the seat to provide a response to the ski just as a ski boot serves a stand-up skier. Short adjustable outriggers are used by the mono skier.

Getting into Ski

Help the student transfer from his wheelchair while stabilizing the mono ski. See bi ski illustration on page 95.

Illustration shows the independent transfer of an accomplished mono skier.

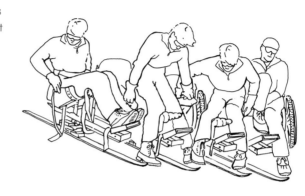

Outrigger Position and Length

With a slight bend in elbow, position the tips of outriggers next to heel of the foot. Use extra brake for beginners. Usage decreases as skier advances.

Instructions to Verify Proper Location of the Ski Under the Mono Ski

1. Mark the Ski: Measure the straight line distance from the tip of the ski to the tail and divide this distance in half. Measure this distance from the tail of the ski forward. Place a permanent mark at mid-cord position on the ski using tape or a permanent marker.

2. Find Balance Point: While in the mono ski, place a wooden dowel underneath the ski at mid-cord. With the dowel in this position the skier should be able to lean forward and the front of the ski should touch the ground. If the seat is appropriately positioned, leaning back should cause the rear of the ski to drop to the ground.

3. Adjust Balance Point: If the balance point does not correspond to the mid-cord position of the ski, it will be necessary to move the seat forward or backward. Once you find the best position for the seat, place a permanent mark on the mono ski frame that corresponds with the mid-cord position of the ski. Adaptive ski programs with mono skis may wish to place permanent marks on the mono ski frame

at 1" intervals. By numbering or lettering those marks, individuals using the equipment will learn which number or letter they will want to correspond with the mid-cord position of any particular ski. This can save a lot of time and eliminates the need to conduct the balance test each time the skier uses the equipment. Having the balance point at the mid-cord position of the ski is a good place to start. With experience you may find that your personal preference dictates that you want your balance point to be slightly in front of or behind the mid-cord position of the ski.

Note: This is a good exercise to introduce angulation. Define center of balance concept, based on trunk position and arm placement.

Body Position and Balance

1. Practice balance with outriggers, next to heel of boot, relaxing arms and keeping elbows unlocked, shoulders relaxed, head up and eyes forward.

2. Rock back and forth. Flat ski to edge and back.

3. Rotate upper body left and right.

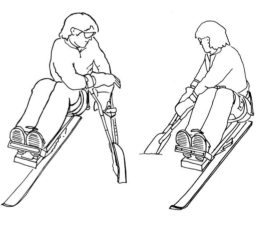

1. Swing arms forward and back together and in opposition.

Fore/Aft Static Rehearsal of Movements Instruct the student on body position as it relates to the mono ski.

Falling Do not try to break the fall. Place outriggers across lap if possible. Another alternative is to hold the outriggers upward at arm's length.

Getting Up, Assisted With the mono ski across the fall line, the instructor places his uphill ski against the mono ski. He then grasps the mono ski and pulls it into an upright position. The safest way is to have the instructor remove skis and straddle the mono ski. Bring the mono ski to an upright position. This can prevent injury to instructor and damage to mono ski.

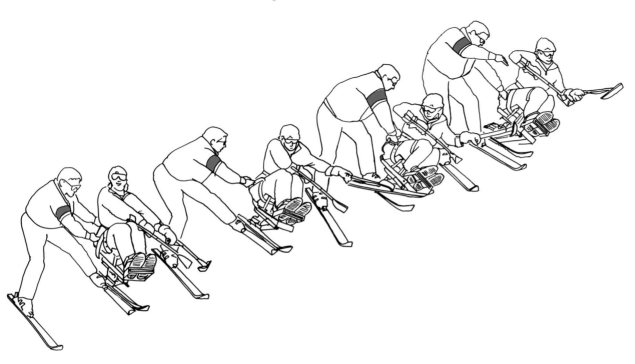

Getting Up, Unassisted

Place the mono ski across the fall line. In the up position both outriggers are placed uphill next to the mono ski. By pushing on the outriggers the mono is brought to an upright position.

Moving on the Flat

Utilizing outriggers push and glide across flat terrain. This can be accomplished with the outriggers in the up position or down position. It is easier for the beginning skier to use the outriggers in the up position.

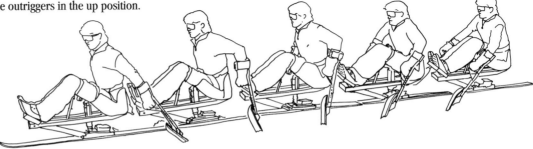

Loading the Triple or Quad Chairlift with Assist

1. The instructor assists in getting the mono ski into position. The student pulls the lever, which elevates the mono ski, making it compatible with the chairlift for loading.

2. Move into position until the back of the mono ski aligns with the "Stand Here" line. Ask the lift attendant to stabilize the chair. As the chairlift approaches, lift the seat portion of the mono ski only, so that the mono ski will slide onto the chair. Triple chairs can be loaded with either a slow or a stop.

3. Secure the mono ski safely onto chair.

4. The instructor fastens the safety line to the back of the chair with carabiner.

Loading Double Chairlift with Assist

One instructor should remove skis and assist the student to the "wait here" line. The other instructor will ride with the student, on the same side as the lift operator, and be the one that communicates with the lift attendant.

It is best to use a stop when loading a double chair, but this depends on the rules of the ski area. If the skier is a beginner, a full stop is advisable.

Unloading Chairlift with Assist

1. ***DO NOT*** remove the safety strap/carabiner until the mono ski is over the unloading ramp. Ask for a slowdown or a stop.

2. The instructors can move the mono ski from side to side. This motion should be done as a "wiggle" to release. Skier leans forward or helper pushes mono ski forward to press tip to ramp and snow to leave the chair. The instructor should always have a firm grasp on the mono ski so that he will not unload too early. Make sure the mono ski points straight down the unload ramp and that the unload is as gentle as possible.

3. As the skier unloads from the chair, there will be a bounce as the mono ski drops onto the spring/ski. The instructor moves the mono ski off the ramp. The skier places the outriggers over his lap.

4. Move the skier away from the unloading ramp.

Independent Loading

Independent loading is similar to assist loading with the following exceptions:

Communication between the mono skier and the lift operators is essential. Coordinate the speed of the chairlift with the ability of the mono skier. Use proper hand signals to slow chair down or to stop. Also, have the lift attendant call top of the lift telling them number of the chair that the mono skier is on.

Timing is important to ensure smooth loading and unloading of the chair lift. With the mono ski in the loading position, the skier looks over his shoulder as the chair lift approaches. As mono ski and chair connect, skier makes sure that mono ski is securely on the chair. Immediately fasten the safety line with a carabiner.

Note: As mono ski and chairlift connect it is sometimes necessary to apply pressure upward on the outriggers to adjust to a variance in the chairlift height.

independent Unloading

As the skier approaches the unloading ramp, he signals to the operator to slow or stop the chair, if necessary. He then unfastens the safety line/carabiner while over the unloading ramp. Just at the lip of the unloading ramp, the skier extends his outriggers forward, causing the mono to now begin to exit the chairlift. He continues down the ramp and moves quickly out of the unloading zone.

Note: While riding the chairlift the skier can extend outriggers upward, hooking outrigger tips on bale of the chairlift. This can create security and helps to stabilize mono ski while on chair.

Chairlift Evacuation

Each ski area has its own evacuation procedures. The best advice here is to stage a mock evacuation with the ski patrol at least once a season, preferably at the beginning of each season. The mono ski and the skier should always be equipped with an evacuation harness that is properly adjusted and secured to the mono ski.

Straight Run to a Braking Stop (Beginning Terrain)

Turn student into fall line.

Assume proper body position.

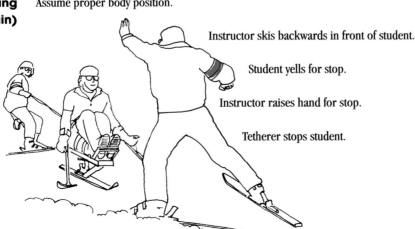

Instructor skis backwards in front of student.

Student yells for stop.

Instructor raises hand for stop.

Tetherer stops student.

Uphill Turn to a Stop with Tether Assist (Beginning Terrain)

Start in a straight run
- Turn head and thumbs in direction of turn.
- If the ski is flat on the snow, the turn will occur.
- Have the skier shift weight slightly forward.
- Open the door with uphill outrigger.
- Steer ski to a skidded stop.

After skier has made a turn to a stop in both directions, move on to beginning linked turns. After the skier has crossed the fall line, have him sit up straight and turn head, shoulders and thumb into the next turn.

Beginning Linked Turns

Keep a flat ski throughout turns. Position body mass over center of ski. Look eyes and shoulders in the direction of turn. Increase the arc of turn as the student improves.

Using a Double Tether to Assist Beginning Turns

If the student is having problems with balance or turning the ski, you may want to try using a double tether. With each end of the tether attached to the sides of the buckets, the tether can help the beginning student remain upright and assist with turns.

Linked Unassisted Turns

Have the student try unassisted turns on a flat ski and making shallow, linked turns in the fall line. He uses his hips to make the weight shift, blocking his shoulders downhill, and the outrigger to initiate the turn. This is comparable to learning to steer a gliding wedge for able-bodied skiers.

Medium-Radius Turns

Begin to close the radius of the turn, no longer traversing the slope. Reduce glide time between turns.

Techniques: Body Angulation

When heading down the fall line, tell the student to keep his head centered, weighting the uphill edge with his hips and/or body weight. Use this to initiate turns. Caution him not to hold too long or skidding will occur. To complete the turn, have him return to centered balance point and glide into fall line with unweighting motion (similar to the angulation of able-bodied skier's ankle, knee and hip).

Balance

Leaning forward helps to initiate a turn and then returning to the center to balance assists in completing turns.

Outrigger Positon

Simultaneous weighting and placing the downhill outrigger forward will initiate a turn. Remind the student to unweight the downhill outrigger to complete the turn and advance the opposite outrigger to initiate the opposite turn (similar to able-bodied skier's pole touch).

Head Position

The head must always be centered and looking down the fall line (able-bodied skier's shoulder/head in a countered placement).

Exercise:
Sideslip

From the fall line, using a flat ski, gradually move to a slight edge and back to a flat ski. Continue this motion using alternating outriggers. Have the skier keep eyes, shoulders down the hill. Use flat terrain. Emphasize rhythm and body position.

Speed Control Tips

- Traverse uphill when needed.
- Wide-radius turns or quicker, faster turns.
- Attempt to remain relaxed.
- Drag tail of outriggers.

Advanced Turns
(Intermediate/
Advanced,
Groomed Trails)

Utilize previously learned skills. All movements are similar but much more aggressive and dynamic. With eyes and shoulders down the fall line, emphasize spine angulation and counter rotation, resulting in refined edge pressure skills. These skills provide a basis to advance into more difficult terrain, such as moguls, steeps and upper-level skiing.

Short-radius skiing involves quicker execution of narrower radius turns in the fall line. Outrigger placement should be closer in toward the mono ski. The lead outrigger is used more to pivot turn as an able-bodied skier's pole plant. Teach the student to push off with the uphill outrigger placed in center position in order to upweight the body. Body position at this ability level depends on a shorter rocking motion of the body. The head is always looking down the fall line and centered shoulders follow the head. Skiers should be cautioned as they start to ski faster and more independently that they could roll the ski. In a roll, tuck the head forward much like in a sit ski to reduce the chance of injury.

Edging

Introduce the edging concept with able-bodied assistance and demonstration by the instructor.

Edge Slip Drill

Sideslip to uphill edge without assistance; repeat across the slope. The student should lead with the downhill outrigger and lean with forward in initiate a turn in a rocking motion, then return to his center of balance. The instructor stresses leaning uphill with the edge into the slope and keeping the head centered. Practice until proficient.

Uphill Christy or
Hockey Stop Drill

A hockey stop is a skidded stop using the uphill edge, perpendicular to the fall line, to make a quick stop. Drill should progress with increased speed; practice until proficient.

Exercise: Falling Leaf

From a sideslip, adjust pressure forward on a flat ski. Open door with downhill outrigger. Keep eyes and shoulders down the fall line; tip of ski will move toward the fall line. Move pressure backward while on a flat ski; tip will turn uphill.

Do above with aft leverage. In a sideslip move fore and aft like a "falling leaf." This exercise is very effective for the advanced skier to develop the commitment to make the turn on a steeper slope.

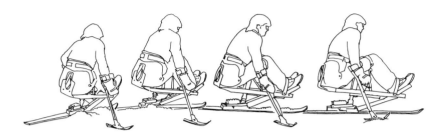

Exercise: Garland

From a static traverse, place the outriggers in a neutral position. Move pressure forward, permitting ski tip to move slightly toward the fall line. Lightly engage the inside edge of ski to create a turn finish. Continue this maneuver several times diagonally across the slope, not completing a turn. Skidding will eventually lead to an uphill christy. Make sure you have good terrain for sideslipping. Repeat in both directions. Also effective for the advanced skier to develop turn initiation.

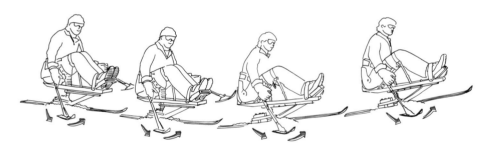

Since moguls vary in shape, size, and snow conditions, it is necessary to ski some bumps defensively and others offensively. Movement patterns are dictated by the bumps. Some ski runs will have bumps with rhythm; others will not. It is necessary to know how to adjust your technique to accommodate the ever-changing terrain.

Skiing moguls can be a great joy, but it can tax your strength and stamina.

Often adaptive equipment is used only in the beginning teaching phases. The goal is to eliminate it as the student progresses.

Bucket

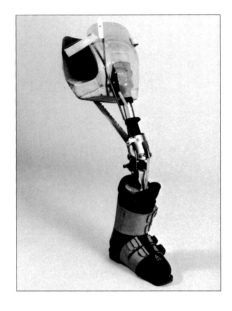

This prosthesis is presently in the experimental stage, to be used by an individual with a hip disarticulation. Hopefully a better design of the hip and knee flexation will soon be available to permit getting onto and off the chairlift. Hip flexation is also used in falling and getting up.

Snow pants protect the prosthesis and keep the lower torso warm.

Bungee Cord Elastic cord.

Bungee and Pipe Length of pipe can be adjusted to accommodate varying needs of the student, including width of wedge. A washer is inserted between ski and knotted bungee.

Bungee Only This allows for more mobility, i.e., sliding into lift line. Length can be adjusted as required. Many students will graduate from using the bungee after the initial learning stages.

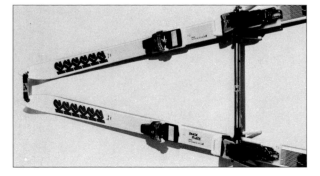

Cant

This plastic wedge is placed under the binding to equalize weight distribution and is available in various thicknesses.

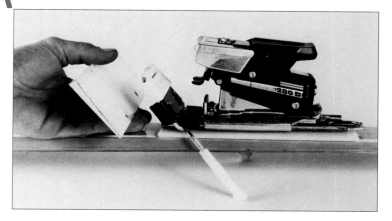

Cant in Boot Under Heel

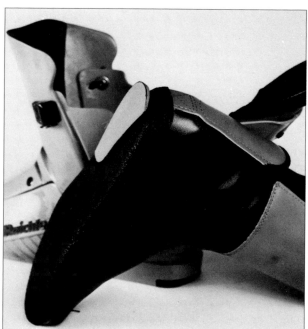

Lift

This wedge, varying in thickness, is intended to increase forward lean. A flat lateral lift should be used under the good leg to keep the hips level. A 1" lift should be the highest used (unless working with a prosthesis); over that height requires a slant board or a plastic wedge under the binding.

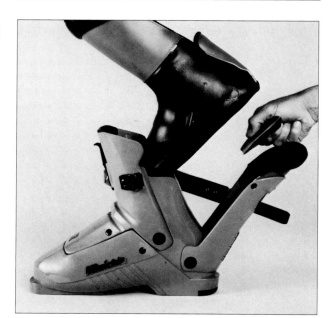

Bi Ski

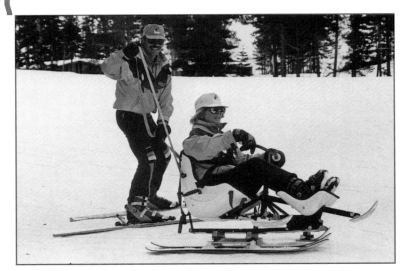

This bi ski is manufactured by Milty, and has a design for both children and adults.

Mono Ski

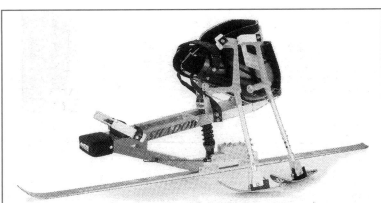

Shadow mono ski

Yetti Mono skis, child and adult

Injuries above a T7 may require a harness for more trunk support and balance.

Outrigger Forearm crutch with 14" ski tip mounted on a rocker base.

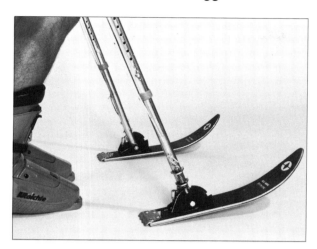

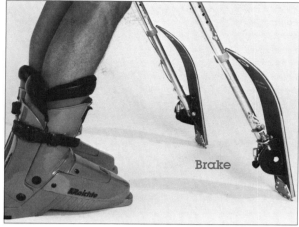

Brake

Sit Ski Sled-type device is used by nonambulatory individuals.

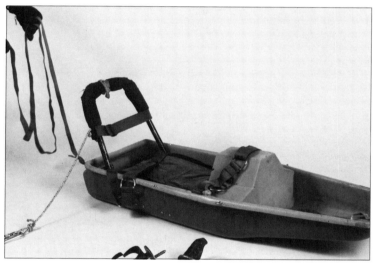

Straps, Picks, Pads and Tetherer's Strap

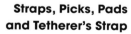

Snow Skirt

Neoprene material is secured around the sit skier and attached to the perimeter of the sit ski for stability and warmth. Evacuation straps are secured by a carabiner. A roll bar is mounted on the back of the sit ski to protect the individual.

Ski Bra Metal device clamped onto the tips of the skis, connected by an eyelet.

Ski Bra Trombone This device is useful for maintaining a parallel position and can slide back and forth to allow for walking and independent leg movements while skiing.

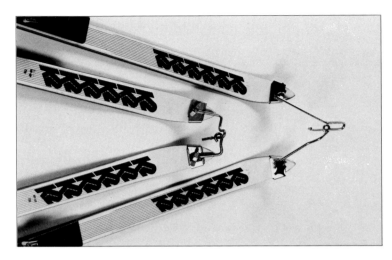

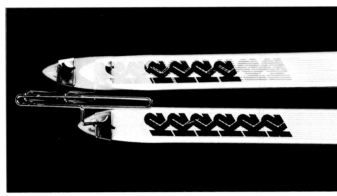

Skier's Safety Strap

The safety strap comes in a number of sizes. The safety strap is placed around the waist. This device is used by skiers who are seizure-prone, autistic or have any of a number of other disabilities.

Since the strap is a safety tool, it is very important that it be in place prior to riding the chairlift.

The safety strap is equipped with a carabiner. While riding the chairlift the carabiner is secured to the chair immediately after loading. It should not be removed until the skier is well over the unloading ramp.

Slant Board

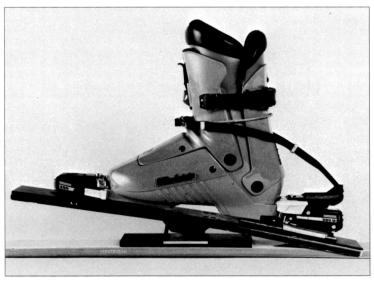

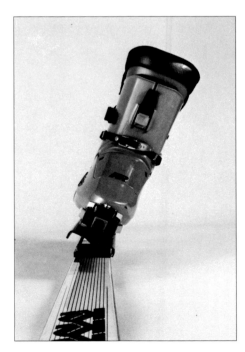

This board with a binding mounted on an adjustable base is used to bring an individual as close as possible to the center of gravity over the ball of the foot. It is shown here in combination with a maximum 4" toe lift, but could also have a maximum 4" heel lift. When the toes are raised, the outriggers must be lengthened accordingly.

Toe Bar (or Toe Spreader)

This may or may not be used with a slant board and is usually permanently mounted to the toe piece. The turnbuckle is telescopic to adjust to various lengths.

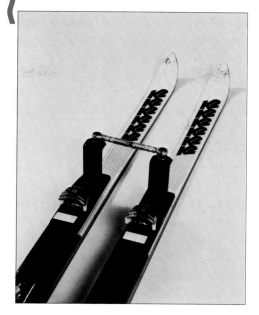

Walker with Sit Ski and Ski Bra

Attach a bungee cord around the boot and the legs of the walker.

Cinch/Reins/Body Harness

This device is used with or without the walker, mainly by children and young adults.

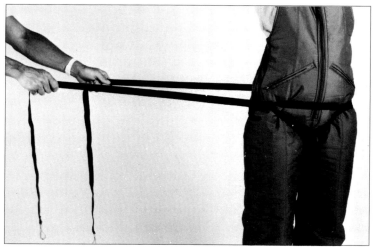

History of the Competition Program

The Competition Program for the Disabled had its beginnings in 1979. Under the direction of Handicap Program instructor Fred Tassone and Winter Park employee Homer Jennings, informal race training was offered to skiers with disabilities eyeing the newly developing U.S. National Championship Series and the U.S. Disabled Ski Team (USDST), sponsored by National Handicapped Sports. In 1981 the program started to gel into a group of hard-core racers living in Winter Park and training, while holding part-time jobs around town. Winter Park Resort was fast becoming the unofficial home of the USDST. Racers in the program were starting to make their mark in national and international competitions.

By 1984 the NHS had developed its National Championships to the point of having racers qualify through a regional race series, and the USDST had become a major power on the international race scene. To keep up with this increased level of competition, both NHS and Winter Park started looking at the possibility of expanding the competition program into a full-scale, structured, season-long training program serving not only the local racers, but also providing much-needed training for developing racers around the country. In September 1984, a proposal was submitted by USDST member Paul DiBello and accepted by Winter Park with the blessing of NHS. A program would be designed to offer ski racers with disabilities structured training time in both a full-season and camp format similar to those offered to all skiers throughout the world.

"Believe in them; it's the experience of a lifetime."

Columbia Crest Cup, Winter Park, Colorado
NHS National Qualifying Series

PHOTO: JOHN WEILAND

The Competition Program Now

The National Sports Center for the Disabled competition program is now a firmly established, high-level training program for over 200 racers around the country, and remains a key developmental training program for skiers seeking their personal best.

For many adaptive skiers the opportunity to compete in ski racing will be their on chance to participate in sports as equals with their peers. The current movement in racing for people with disabilities is to encourage young racers to compete in the well-established United States Ski Association (USSA) amateur race series as well as in ski races for people with disabilities.

Annual Summer Training Camp, Cardrona Ski Resort, Wanaka, New Zealand

Competition coaching programs should seek to model themselves as closely to traditional programs as possible, working on sound foundations and building race techniques and tactics. Sound coaching philosophy emphasizes working the disabled racer in the above progression as close to accepted nondisabled coaching progressions as possible. Modifications of progressions or actual techniques are then incorporated for the various disabilities.

A program coach is a good coach first and foremost; the nuances of techniques and racing for people with disabilities in general are quickly learned.

Paul DiBello
Program Director

The following is excerpted from USSA's competition guide and covers the disabled classification system for both national and international competition. Racers should be aware that more emphasis will be placed on "USSA Points" in the future.

Disabled Competition Rules

At the international level, races are sanctioned by the FIS (International Ski Federation). All racing in the U.S. is conducted according to USSA and FIS rules. There are some minor modifications, but these are of a technical nature and do not affect course and hill specifications. As an example of the ability level, speeds of 70 mph are now common in downhill competitions. Racers are not seeded by points but rather by draw within the various classes. A skier is classified based on two factors: (1) disability, and (2) method of skiing. The classification categories shown should be helpful in explaining this procedure.

National Disabled Ski Classifications

Alpine Classes	Equipment	Disability
LW1	4 Track	disability of both legs, skiing with outriggers and using two skis or skiing on one ski using a prosthesis
LW2	3 Track	disability of one leg, skiing with outriggers and one ski, using poles instead of outriggers is allowed
LW3	2 skis w/poles	disability of both legs
LW4	2 skis w/poles	disability of one leg
LW5/7	2 skis w/o poles	disability of both arms or hands
LW6/8	2 skis w/1 pole	disability in one arm or hand
LW9		disability of a combination of arm and leg using equipment of their choice
LW10	Mono ski	disability of both legs that does not allow the skier to compete in a standing position
LW11	Mono ski	disability of both legs that does not allow the skier to compete in a standing position
LW12	Mono ski	disability of both legs that does not allow the skier to compete in a standing position

*Classification into LW10, 11 or 12 is based on a functional test, LW10 being for the more severely disabled and LW12 for those of lesser disability.

B1	Totally blind	can distinguish between light and dark, but not shapes
B2	Partially sighted	best correctable vision up to 20/600 and/or visual field of 5 degrees
B3	Partially sighted	best correctable vision from 20/600 to 20/200 and/or field of vision from 5 degrees to -20 degrees

"When they are on the slopes, they are on the same level as all the other skiers and looked up to by many as having the courage to attempt to ski, let alone compete."

These definitions are intended to provide a common base for discussions and instruction of skiing and to make communicating with students easier. By no means should the instructor insist on using them if it becomes obvious that the students do not understand what is being said. Because we are using words with meanings specific to our sport, which may have a different common language meaning, students may have no idea what we are talking about. When in doubt, have the students repeat what you just said in their own words to see if they understand. More often than not, you will be surprised by what was actually heard. Precise use of words may be necessary, however, for technical discussions among instructors.

abilities
basic building blocks, depending on both genetic and learning factors, used in the development of skills (not synonymous with skills).

absorption
flexion/extension movements of the body to absorb and even out the pressure variations on the skis that result from the dynamics of the turn or terrain variations.

alignment
to bring into line, eliminate a twisted relationship of one part of the body with respect to another.

angulating
moving on a diagonal and/or lateral plane in a flexing or extending fashion. Angulating and angulation imply bending or extending movements in the feet, knees, spine and any combination thereof.

anticipation
a movement in preparation for turning, during which upper and lower body segments are brought into a twisted relationship. The muscles that are stretched as a result are quicker and stronger in contracting and causing movement.

ATS
an abbreviation for the American Teaching System, an entire teaching/learning system including the underlying philosophy and the mechanical movement progressions required to facilitate learning how to ski. ATS rests strongly on a humanistic, participatory teaching/learning philosophy.

balancing
the action of maintaining equilibrium. "Static balance" refers to a state involving an equilibrium of forces and movements while the person is not in motion. "Dynamic balance" refers to equilibrium while in motion.

cants
wedge-shaped devices placed under bindings to change the orientation of the boots and legs with respect to the skis.

carving
turning the skis with little lateral movement of the skis over the snow. In principle, when the skis execute a pure carved turn, each point of the ski edge passes over the same point in the snow, leaving a distinct, sharp line in the snow. The reality is that turns are skidded to a greater or lesser degree; therefore, "skidding" is the generic term for direction changes when the skis are in contact with the snow. If the turn involves a large amount of skidding, it may come closer to a "slipping" turn; if less skidding, it will be closer to a "carved" turn. Movement on skis will involve the full range, from slipping to carving, and each form of direction change can be useful and desirable depending on the circumstances.

center of mass   that point of the body where, for analysis of the dynamics of movement, all of the body's mass may be considered to reside. Usually this point is in the region of the navel; as the body flexes and assumes different postures, the center of mass moves around. Also called center of gravity.

checking   the action of slowing or stopping skidding of the skis on the snow. When linking turns, checking usually involves tightening the turn radius. The resulting rebound action may aid in entering the new turn.

christy   a turn during which the skis skid at some time on corresponding edges. (Corresponding means both left or both right edges, as viewed by the skier.)

cognitive   the process of knowing; knowledge or the capacity for it.

counter rotation   the movement of twisting the torso and legs in opposite directions concurrently.

crossover   moving the body's center of mass forward and over the skis from the inside of one turn to the inside of the next turn.

cross-under   moving the feet and the skis under the body's center of mass from the outside of one turn to the outside of the next turn.

edge angle   the degree of tilt of the ski about its longitudinal axis in relation to the snow's surface.

edge change   the action of tilting from one edge to the other. This action is the most fundamental aspect of turning. It can be performed while the skis are in contact with the snow or it can be performed without such contact.

edge control   the action of adjusting the edge angle to the task at hand.

equilibrium   (state of balance) means that the person maintains a desired posture (e.g., upright) while in motion down the hill. This concept should be understood to mean maintaining a desired posture under different disturbances whether standing still, moving slowly over smooth surfaces or rapidly over rough, uneven snow.

extension   any movement resulting in an increase of a joint angle (e.g., the angle between two adjacent parts of a limb).

exteroceptive   stimuli acting on the body from without, as in touch, smell or sight.

fall line   the imaginary line that follows the greatest angle of the slope. Through any point on the hill, there is at least one fall line.

flexion   any movement resulting in a decrease of a joint angle.

four track   two skis and two outriggers.

garland   a series of direction changes that do not lead the skier to reverse direction across the fall line. (A direction change is to be understood as a deviation from a straight-line motion.)

guidance something that guides. Although synonymous with steering, guidance here implies a somewhat more subtle action.

guide to direct motion by physical action; to use muscular movement to direct motion.

hip projection a movement of the hips forward or to the side to produce up unweighting or to impart lateral momentum. This movement is distinguished from the movement of hip rotation, which is discussed below. Hip projection may be used to augment rotary movement to start a turn.

hip rotation generating rotary momentum by slowing or stopping a turning movement of the hips. Sometimes referred to as "blocking" the turning movement of the hips.

hockey stop simultaneous turning of the skis abruptly while using forward pressure and edge control to a sudden stop.

hop turn utilized solely by the three track skier. Introduced as a beginning maneuver to change direction and to familiarize the student with his equipment. Also assists in changing direction during the beginning traverse phase.

inclination deviation from a vertical body position. This term is usually used to describe the overall appearance of the body in relationship to a vertical reference.

initiation phase of a turn that phase of a turn during which changing from edge to edge allows a direction change to be started. In this context, direction change means a turn where one starts with one edge engaged and completes the turn with the opposite edge engaged.

leverage applying pressure in front of or behind the midpoint of the skis; the deliberate adjustment of the pressure distribution on the skis to exploit the design of the skis to aid in turning. This application may result in either the tip or the tail of the ski being more heavily pressured. The actions do not necessarily imply overall body lean, either forward or backward. Such actions can be used, but leverage can also be the result of more subtle body motions (such as knee flexion) or a result of dynamics (such as terrain use or acceleration/deceleration of the entire body).

matching the movement toward aligning the direction of the skis after they have been brushed or stepped into a wedge position. Matching implies that the skis are brought either from positions of divergence or convergence toward a parallel relationship.

method the process whereby a sport is taught. Methodology is the overall approach to, or orderly arrangement of, the process of teaching various movement options.

open stance parallel turns simultaneous steering of both skis followed by the rotation of the legs and skidding of the skis. Skier assumes parallel stance throughout the progression of the turn.

outrun unobstructed natural run-out of the terrain that allows student to come to a full stop.

platform setting the edge after skidding or slipping to provide a basis for future action, such as rebound.

pole touch initiates a turn and encourages rhythm, edge control and weight shift.

preparation phase that phase of the turn during which the prerequisites to start a turn are performed. When analyzing the flow of movements, the preparation phase for one turn is also the finishing phase of the preceding turn. The combination of these actions and functions is essential to linking turns smoothly.

pressure control the action of actively adjusting the pressure between the skis and the snow. Active pressure control will involve such actions as increasing or decreasing the pressure on the front, back or middle of the skis, use of leverage exerted by the lower legs against the boots and bindings or body lean. Other mechanisms can involve vertical or lateral displacements of the body mass through muscular actions, for example, as the result of flexion or extension. Where the pressure on the skis is distributed will be determined by a combination of these body movements and the dynamics of the situation.

proprioceptive stimuli produced within the body by internal movements.

rebounding the recoil, or effect of springing back, in response to the forces of compression exerted on the body, the skis and the snow.

retraction the action of pulling the legs up under the body by contracting the muscles of the abdomen and hips. This movement is used to absorb pressure increases due to terrain changes or the effects of turn dynamics.

rotary initiation the process of transmitting the rotary momentum of the torso and the hips around the vertical body axis to the feet and the skis. Torque is transmitted when the rotary movement of the torso and hips is slowed or stopped.

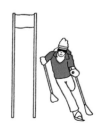

rotary push-off a mechanism of pushing off from one or both feet in a manner that imparts a rotary motion to the body about its vertical axis.

short swing linked short-radius turns utilizing anticipation and pivoted rebound.

sideslipping a slipping motion straight down the fall line.

sidestepping means of climbing hill in beginning phases by having ski(s) perpendicular to fall line and utilizing uphill edge of ski.

skidding the composite result of the skis moving forward and sideways simultaneously.

sliding the movement of the skis in the direction of the longitudinal axis.

slipping a movement sideways. This sideways movement can occur with the skis perpendicular to the line of motion or at some other orientation to the line of travel of the skier/skis.

skills the proficiency in a specific task or limited group of tasks. Skill level depends on a certain collection of basic abilities, past experiences and type and duration of practice.

steering actively directing the path of the skis by muscular actions.

tactics the skillful methods used to gain a desired objective.

technique the choice made among the movement options available to accomplish a given goal.

tetherer an individual who skis behind the sit ski using a tether line, which is attached to the sit ski for safety purposes.

three track one ski and two outriggers.

touch system used to assist students to assume a proper ski position by touching the knees, hips, etc.

traversing moving in a direction that deviates from the fall line.

turning the action of reorienting the body's direction of travel; a change in the path of the center of mass.

two point hold accomplished by using the following steps:
1. Work from behind the student;
2. The instructor positions one ski between the student's skis and the other ski on the outside;
3. Place the outside hand below the knee of the student and the other hand on the student's shoulder or hip, depending on which feels more comfortable for instructional purposes.

For people with disabilities, the two point hold position can serve as an important tool in teaching control, assisting in turning and in stopping. This maneuver should eventually lead to the student becoming independent of the instructor.

uphill christy simultaneous steering of both skis into the hill while skidding to a complete stop.

wedge equal displacement of the tails of the skis, forming a "piece of pie."

weighting/ unweighting pressure control to achieve weight transfer.

* Excerpts reprinted with permission of the Professional Ski Instructors of America from *Strategies for Teaching: American Teaching System*, P.S.I.A., Publishers Press, Salt Lake City, Utah. © 1987 and *American Teaching System: Alpine Skiing*, P.S.I.A., © 1993.

Terms of Movement

Flexion	bending
Extension	straightening
Abduction	movement away from the midline
Adduction	movement toward the midline
Pronation	rotate hand or forearm so as to bring palm facing downward
Supination	clockwise rotation of hand or forearm, palm facing upward
Internal rotation	rotation toward the midline
External rotation	rotation away from the midline
Inversion	turning inward, toward the midline. As a treatment technique, head lower than feet.
Eversion	turning outward, away from the midline
Rotation	as a treatment technique, twisting trunk off of hips
Motor patterns	the ways in which the body and limbs work together to make movement possible
Sensorimotor experience	the feelings of one's own movement

Areas and Bones of the Body

Axilla	under the arm	
Scapular region	area around the shoulder blades	
Pectoral region	front of the chest	
Shoulder girdle (bones of)	Scapula	shoulder blades
	Clavicle	collarbone
Sternum	breast bone	
Humerus	upper arm bone	
Forearm	extends from elbow to wrist	
Radium	one of the two bones of the forearm (thumb side)	
Ulna	one of the two bones of little finger side	
Carpal bones	eight bones of the wrist	
Metacarpal bones	five bones in the hand, corresponding with the five fingers	
Phalanges	bones of the fingers or toes	
Pollex	thumb	
Trunk	body	
Gluteal region	hip and buttock	
	Hip bone	Ilium—large upper part, felt in lower margin of waist
	Ischium	lower part of which body rests in sitting position
	Pubis	anterior part, bone felt at lower part of front of abdomen
	Pelvic girdle	two hip bones together
	Iliac crest	bony ridge below waist
	Femur	thigh bone
	Acetabulum	cavity in hip bone that receives head of femur
	Patella	kneecap
	Inguinal region	groin
	Tibia	shin bone
	Fibula	calf bone
	Malleolus	ankle bone (protuberances on both sides of ankle joint)
	Tarsal bones	seven bones of the ankle
	Metatarsal bones	five bones in the foot
	Hallux	big toe
	Spinal column	consists of 33 vertebrae:
		7 Cervical vertebrae
		12 Thoracic vertebrae
		5 Lumbar vertebrae
		5 Sacral vertebrae
		4 Coccygeal vertebrae

Amyotrophic Lateral Sclerosis

Amyotrophic Lateral Sclerosis (ALS), sometimes known as Lou Gehrig's disease, is a crippling, fatal neuromuscular disease that strikes people between 35 and 65. It is more common in men than women. ALS is a progressive disease that attacks the motor neurons, the nerve cells that control movement of the voluntary muscles, causing their disintegration. The damage weakens muscles responsible for swallowing, speech, chewing, the limb muscle, and eventually the breathing muscles. Throughout the disease intelligence and the senses are not affected.

The symptoms usually start with weakness in the arms or legs, or may start with difficulty speaking or swallowing. Many people develop muscle spasms and cramps as well as loss of muscle mass. Since this is a progressive disease, people will eventually experience all of the symptoms and virtually all of the body's muscles will be affected within two to five years. In some people the disease progresses slowly, even up to 10 to 20 years after diagnosis.

There is no known cause, although many theories are being investigated, including that it is from a faulty immune system or environmental toxins. There is no cure. Most people are treated with medications to lessen the symptoms, like muscle relaxants and antispasmotics. Mobility devices aid in ambulation. Making changes in food preparation for easy-to-swallow foods and eventually a respirator are used when it becomes difficult to breathe.

Aphasia

A patient with aphasia may have difficulty understanding or producing any form of language. What he hears or reads may be meaningless. He may be unable to think of the words he wants to say. His speech may not always be meaningful or express a complete thought. Writing is usually not an alternative to speaking as most aphasics have just as much difficulty trying to write words as they do saying them.

When communicating with an aphasic person, it is helpful to use both words and gestures to help him understand what you are talking about. Use short, simple sentences but do not "talk down" to him. Speak in a normal tone of voice. Aphasics are not deaf but merely have difficulty understanding the meaning of the words they hear. Try to ask questions that do not require a choice. "Do you want to go to bed?" is better than "Do you want to go to bed or stay up and watch TV?" Give the person time to answer as best he can before continuing on to another question. If the person cannot think of the word, encourage him to show you what he needs. The patient's speech pathologist can give you specific suggestions for the best means of communicating with him.

Loss of language does not mean the person is less intelligent. Having aphasia is a bit like trying to communicate in a foreign country when you can only say or understand a few words of the language.

At times an aphasic may laugh or cry more easily or inappropriately. This is due to lability, which is lack of emotional control. Excessive or unexpected swearing may be present.

Arthritis

Arthritis is an inflammatory disease of the joints and other parts of the body. It is actually more than 100 different diseases and affects one in every seven people of all ages. It is a serious disease causing pain and loss of movement and function, and in some types major disability. Once acquired, it lasts a lifetime, although there may be periods of remission. Each type is different and has a different cause.

Some types are: rheumatoid arthritis, osteoarthritis, systemic lupus erythematosus, scleroderma, gout, juvenile arthritis, ankylosing spondylitis, psoriatic arthritis, infectious arthritis, fibrositis, bursitis, tendinitis, osteoporosis, Lyme disease, reflex sympathetic dystrophy syndrome, Paget's disease, carpal tunnel syndrome, Raynaud's syndrome, the Marfan syndrome and immobility-caused osteoarthritis.

The common symptom of arthritis is inflammation, which damages healthy tissues of the body. Damage occurs in the bones and other tissues of the joints, causing loss of movement, stiffness, swelling, difficulty of movement and even deformity of the areas affected. The most common chronic disabling forms of arthritis are:

Osteoarthritis: This is the most common type of arthritis. Although thought to be a disease of the old, it is a common side effect of immobility. This means that anyone with a disability or disabling disease is susceptible, primarily in the weak or affected body part. It is a degenerative disease of the joints that can affect any joint, but most common are the fingers, knees, hips and spine. Both overuse and long periods of immobilizing the joints affected aggravate the symptoms.

Juvenile arthritis: This is a general term for any kind of arthritis that affects children, from rheumatoid arthritis, lupus, ankylosing spondylitis, to any other form. Each type is different and varies from the adult form of the disease. These conditions can be very serious and can include symptoms of the underlying disease plus: skin rash, inflammation of the eyes, fever, slowed growth, lymph node enlargement, fatigue and pain and swelling of the muscles and joints.

Ankylosing spondylitis: This is a chronic inflammation of the spine, causing the bones of the spine to fuse together. Motion is limited depending on the area(s) of fusion. Most common is fusion of the neck and/or hips. It may also affect the shoulders, knees and ankles. Fatigue, lung or heart problems and eye inflammation may also be present.

Gout: Gout is an extremely painful form of arthritis caused by a buildup of uric acid in the body. The uric acid crystals appear in a joint, usually a big toe, but can be in any joint, causing inflammation. This is one type of arthritis that can be controlled with diet and medication.

Rheumatoid arthritis (RA): Of all the types of arthritis, this is the most severe and potentially disabling. It is considered to be an autoimmune disease where white blood cells move from the blood into the joint tissues. Joints fill with fluid and the white blood cells. Antibodies are formed that take part in damaging the joint lining, cartilage, bone, tendons and ligaments. This can lead to deformity and related disability, which can be permanent. This is a disease that affects more than the joints. Other symptoms can include any or all of the following: fever, loss of appetite, weight loss, low energy, extreme fatigue, stiffness, achy pain all over, anemia, rheumatoid nodules or lumps over bony areas, inflammation of the lining of the heart and lungs, inflammation of lung tissue, dry eyes, dry mouth, low white blood cell count and rarely inflammation of the blood vessels, vasculitis, which causes problems with other organs, the skin and nerves.

Anyone can develop RA, including children and senior citizens, but it is most common in women (3 to 1), developing from young to middle adulthood. In some people the disease has periods of flare-up, when it is worse, and remissions. In others the disease progresses over time without any periods of remission. There is no cure, and the treatment varies from other forms of arthritis. Some of the medications used in RA include one or more of the following: gold therapy (injections of gold salts); nonsteroidal antiinflammatory drugs; corticoidsteroids given over time and sometimes injected into affected joints; antimalarial drugs; immunosuppressive drugs like Imuran; some anticancer drugs, like Methotrexate and Cytoxan; Azulfidine, D-Penicillamine and analgesics. Many of these medications have serious side effects and need to be monitored closely. Medications should be balanced with healthy lifestyle changes. A balance of rest and exercise, avoiding extreme cold, aquatic exercise, range of motion of affected joints as well as healthy ones, rest when the disease is most active and exercise when the disease settles down, physical and occupational therapy, maintaining a healthy diet, and stress management techniques are all useful in staying as healthy as possible with this disease. Sometimes total joint replacement is useful.

General therapies used for arthritis: Each kind of arthritis has different types of medications that are useful. Common to most types are antiinflammatories. Other things that help are: exercise, rest and relaxation techniques, use of heat or cold, adaptive and self-help aids, joint protection and sometimes surgery.

Asthma, which is also known as a reactive airway disease, is defined as a chronic lung condition with: (1) Inflammation of the airways; (2) increased sensitivity of the airways to a variety of triggers that can cause narrowing of the airways—the major triggers include allergy, exercise, upper respiratory infections and irritants such as cigarette smoke, perfumes and other strong odors; (3) obstruction of airflow which leads to breathing difficulty.

Asthma Early warning signs are experienced before the start of an asthmatic episode. Examples of early warning signs are: feeling tired, itchy throat, runny nose, tightness in chest and headache. Asthma symptoms indicate that an episode is occurring. Action should be taken to treat these symptoms before they become severe. Asthma symptoms include: wheezing, coughing, shortness of breath and an increase in the feeling of tightness in the chest. Severe asthma symptoms are a life-threatening emergency. Examples of severe asthma symptoms include: severe coughing; wheezing; shortness of breath or tightness in the chest; difficulty with concentration or talking; shallow, slow or fast breathing; posturing (hunched shoulders), nasal flaring and cyanosis (gray or bluish tint to skin, beginning around the mouth). Treatment for the asthmatic has advanced significantly since the early 1980s. Corticosteroids are the most common antiinflaminory drugs for the treatment of asthma. Inhaled steroids are often used as a "first-line" drug. Other medications for the treatment of asthma are: Triamcinolone, Flunisolide, Beclomethasone, Beta-agonists, Theophyline, Prednisone, Methylprednisolone and Chromolyn.

Attention Deficit Disorders (ADD) are thought to be neurological in origin-caused by a deficiency in "neurotransmittors," the chemicals that either send or stop messages relayed in the brain. A child who has ADD is of normal or better intelligence and has symptoms that include: easy distractibility, short attention span and impulsive behavior, which may or may not include hyperactivity. While ADD causes many secondary emotional and behavioral problems, it is a physical, not emotional or psychiatric disease. About 10 percent of all school-aged children develop ADD and the incidence is 10:1, more common in males. There are two types of ADD, the first, ADHD (Attention Deficit Hyperactive Disorder), includes hyperactivity, and

Attention Deficit Disorders

the second, Undifferentiated Attention Deficit Disorder (UADD), which is passive in nature. In ADHD, a child tends to be always in trouble, is easily frustrated, has difficulty finishing tasks, doesn't respond to normal discipline, seems to need immediate gratification, is impulsive and unpredictable, can be destructive and aggressive, has difficulty concentrating and following directions, is easily confused if asked to do two things simultaneously, has difficulty sitting still, may engage in actions dangerous to self and may show excessive and inappropriate fear to new and changing situations. A child with UADD tends to be very inattentive, absent-minded and has many problems with organization and distractibility. This child seems very passive and is often underdiagnosed. Both types of children tend to have low self-esteem and great difficulty in school. Adolescents with ADD have additional problems like depression, pregnancy risk, drug abuse, alcohol abuse, antisocial behavior and delinquency.

Children with ADD are treated with psychostimulant medications like Ritalin, Cylert and Dexedrine, as well as behavior modification techniques for the child and the family. When dealing with these children avoid distracting stimuli, only give one direction at a time, maintain eye contact during instructions, simplify complex directions, make all directions as clear and concise as possible, give only one task at a time, give extra time for each task and remember that these children are easily frustrated so maintain a calm attitude with each child. ADD children respond best when dealt with on a one-to-one basis.

Autism is a bioneurological disorder, not a mental illness, that affects the functioning of the brain. Current theories indicate that it may be caused by genetics, viral and/or chemical exposure. It causes a lifelong developmental disability involving problems with communication, social interaction and physical activities. It is usually diagnosed during the first three years of life. In the past, many professionals thought that children with autism (as much as 80 percent) had mental retardation; however, this view is now changing considerably. It has been found that giving the child higher educational expectations has had many favorable results.

Autism

The major characteristics include slowness in understanding messages; problems of the sensory system (inappropriate use of touch, taste and smell), hearing and language disorders (including in some the inability to speak); uneven physical skills appropriate to their age; inappropriate social responses (like screaming, unprovoked tantrums, laughing, crying, echoing other people's words, resisting touch, cuddling and eye contact); sleep disturbances; and in severe forms the child may injure himself, do repetitive or aggressive actions, constantly move various body parts, engage in destructive behavior, show an apparent insensitivity to pain and/or completely isolate himself from all others including parents. Some children have eating disorders and/or seizures.

There is no cure for autism, but there is a wide variety of treatments that have been affective. Most children need a combination of most of the options, which include: intensive and frequent vision, speech, physical and occupational therapies; audi-tory integration therapy; social skill training; behavioral programs; exercise; music; movement; dance; horseback riding therapy; medications; in some cases megavitamin therapy (using vitamin B6, magnesium and DMG) in combination with diets that eliminate possible food allergies has been beneficial.

Some persons with autism use a number of assistive technologies that aid in communication with others. Whether they do or not, it is helpful when dealing with a person with autism to assume that mental competence exists, and to communicate appropriately.

Bipolar Disorders

The initial episode that required hospitalization is usually manic behavior. Both the manic and major depressive episodes are more frequent than the major depressive episodes in major depression. Frequently, a major depressive episode is immediately followed by a short episode of the other kind. Often, two or more complete cycles (a manic and a major depressive episode that succeed each other without a period of remission) can occur within a year. These cases are called "rapid cycling." Rarely, over long periods of time, the two kinds of episodes alternate with no intervening period of normal mood. Evidence shows that cases of bipolar disorder with a mixed or rapid cycling episode have a more chronic course than those without this type of episode. From .4 percent to .2 percent of the adult population have had bipolar disease. Studies show that the disorder is equally common in males and females and occurs at much higher rates in first-degree biological relatives of people with bipolar disorder than in the general population.

Brain Injury

See Traumatic Brain Injury.

Cancer: Leukemia and Sarcoma

Cancer is characterized by abnormal and uncontrolled growth of cells. Cells are tiny structures that make up all parts of the body. All cells reproduce themselves by dividing. Normal growth and repair of tissue take place in this orderly manner. When cell division is not orderly and controlled, abnormal growth occurs. A mass of tissue called a tumor builds up. A tumor may be benign or malignant. A malignant tumor is a cancer.

Leukemia is a cancer of the bone marrow. The bone marrow is the spongy tissue filling the center core of bones and the source of the body's blood. Sarcoma is a cancer of the connective tissue.

A malignant tumor, or cancer, invades neighboring tissues and organs and can spread to other parts of the body, forming new growths called metastases. If cancer cells have spread before a tumor is removed, the disease can recur.

The three main methods of treating cancer are: (1) surgery, (2) radiation therapy and (3) chemotherapy (treatment with anticancer drugs). In many cases treatment consists of two or all three of these methods, a procedure called combination therapy. Both leukemia and sarcoma are treated with chemotherapy.

Anticancer drugs can kill cancer cells in most parts of the body but can also act on normal cells. Even though children in such treatment may look healthy, be aware that they may be more tired and more apt to bruise and hurt, develop infections and become weak. They may be depressed and have an altered mood. There may be partial or total hair loss, the blood count may drop below normal and resistance to infection may be lowered. Some patients undergoing chemotherapy experience diarrhea, nausea, vomiting and loss of appetite. Small ulcers may form in the mouth.

Caution should be taken with different types of sarcoma surgery (amputation of extremities). The amputation may still have a tumor, making a fracture in that area a possibility.

Cerebral Palsy

Cerebral palsy (CP) is a term that describes any disorder of movement and posture that results from a nonprogressive abnormality of the immature brain. Damage to the brain may occur before birth, during delivery or immediately after birth—usually as a result of deprivation of oxygen to the brain. The condition of cerebral palsy can also occur in young children who sustain trauma and resultant injury of the brain.

The brain is the control center from which all body function, thoughts and psychological processes are controlled. Different areas of the brain control different functions: e.g., movement, speech, learning, judgment, hearing, vision, emotions, to name only a few. The area and degree of damage to the brain determine the resultant disability. Often, in addition to damage to the movement area of the brain, other areas are affected. Therefore, more than one of the functions previously listed may be affected in the individual with cerebral palsy. In all cases, the characteristics of abnormal muscle tone, a delay in normal development and abnormal reflex activity are seen.

Physically, cerebral palsy is classified as one or a combination of the following: (1) spastic (tense, contracted muscles); (2) athetoid (extraneous, uncontrolled movements), (3) ataxic (jerky, uncontrolled movements); (4) rigid (stiff, uncontrolled movements) and (5) flaccid (reduced, diminished muscle tone). These vary in degree or severity, from the minimally involved individual, who can function without much evidence of abnormal movement, to the severely involved individual, who has minimal active muscle control and is noted to be controlled by significant abnormal muscle tone.

Cerebral palsy is a lifelong condition that does not get worse except by the general aging process that everyone experiences. In a normal child development occurs at a steady pace. Most children speak and walk by the age of two or three. Dexterity and mental acuity develop over childhood so that by the age of 18 most children have reached adult dexterity, thinking process and movements. In many cases of CP, the development stages from infancy to full adulthood are extended. Many individuals are still developing in their 30s to 50s. So assuming that the person with CP is "stuck" at a certain level of skill may be detrimental to their health."

Management for cerebral palsy often includes physical therapy, occupational therapy, speech therapy, medication, orthopedic management of surgery and/or bracing and other special aids such as wheelchairs, adaptive aids, hearing aids and so forth. As with other neurological disorders, learning disabilities, social immaturity and emotional needs can play an important part in the overall management of each person with cerebral palsy. Communication at an effective level is critical. Most people with CP are not mentally retarded, unless the initiating cause (like trauma) caused more damage than the CP. Even though speech may sometimes be severely affected, it has no bearing on the intelligence of the individual.

Generally speaking, instability is a significant factor in limiting functional movement in cerebral palsy. Abnormal postures and positioning are heightened with higher-level and more stressful physical activities. Abnormal patterns should not be reinforced. Instead, adapt the activity to provide the needed stability in order to gain success in movement.

Chronic Fatigue Syndrome

Chronic fatigue syndrome (CFS) is a mysterious disease that lasts six months to life and has as its main characteristic debilitating and constant fatigue with additional symptoms that vary in individuals. The cause is unknown, although in some individuals it seems to follow an illness like the flu, a virus or infectious mononucleosis. However, many people develop this disease gradually with no preceding illness. Some theories about the cause have been focused on a viral cause, an immune disorder and possibly a hormonal or neurological origin. There are many diseases that have chronic fatigue as a symptom, like multiple sclerosis, systemic lupus, rheumatoid arthritis, post polio syndrome and most other autoimmune diseases, cancers, infections, anemia, AIDS and diseases of the heart, lungs, thyroid, liver, kidneys, gastrointestinal system, endocrine disorders and even depression. Because of this it is a difficult disease to diagnose, as all other possible diseases must be excluded.

The symptoms include debilitating fatigue, with the presence of at least eight of the following: sore throat, low-grade fever, generalized muscle weakness, swollen and painful lymph nodes, muscle aches, headaches, prolonged fatigue after activities and exercise, joint pain, changes in sleep patterns, depression, difficulty in expressing ideas and/or making decisions and vague neurological complaints like numbness, altered sensations and oversensitivity. This syndrome affects anyone at any age and can have major consequences on an individual's life. Some people can no longer work or go to school, and become severely disabled to the extent that they can no longer care for themselves, while others have this disorder for a year or two and it disappears. Unfortunately there is no treatment or medication that has proven effective, although currently many drugs are being researched. What helps the most seems to be teaching the person affected to balance rest, activity along with a balanced diet and general physical conditioning. Antiinflammatories are used to help some of the symptoms, like fever, headache and muscle aches and pains. Also, low doses of tricyclic antidepressants, like Sinequan, seem to help many of the symptoms.

Chronic Illness Caused Disability

Chronic illnesses that cause disability and/or involve chronic fatigue are very different than other disabilities. Injury disabilities are usually caused by a onetime event, with rehabilitation and recovery. After recovery, if there is no underlying disease process, the disabled person is able to use other healthy body parts just as he did previous to the injury. In a chronic illness the entire body is affected. Often the individual may look very "normal" and even "healthy," as the symptoms are frequently "invisible." The types of diseases that fit under this category are: multiple sclerosis, myasthenia gravis, systemic lupus erythematosus, rhematoid arthritis, reflex sympathetic dystrophy syndrome, chronic fatigue syndrome, post stroke patients, post polio syndrome, Guillain-Barré syndrome, cancer patients, heart disease, diabetes, some seizure disorders, Parkinson's disease, Lou Gehrig's disease, postviral syndromes, some metabolic and endocrine disorders (like hypothyroidism) and many others. The major problem with chronic diseases is that the individual often starts out a day with overwhelming fatigue and limited energy resources, making any kind of physical activity a challenge. The person must be able to learn energy conservation techniques in balancing rest with exercise.

Cyclothymia

Cyclothymia is characterized as a chronic mood disturbance of at least two year's duration for adults, one year for children and adolescents. The disorder involves numerous hypomanic episodes and periods of depressed mood and loss of interest or pleasure. To be diagnosed with this disorder, a two-year period for adults (one for children and adolescents) must be determined when the person is never without hypomanic or depressive symptoms for more than two months. If there is clear evidence of either a manic episode or a major depressive episode during the years of the disturbance, this would indicate a diagnosis of bipolar disorder. The boundaries between cyclothymia and bipolar disorder are not clear and some researchers think that cyclothymia is a mild form of bipolar disorder.

Developmental Disabilities

The population of persons with developmental disabilities living in the United States is estimated to be about 10 million. Their disabilities are caused by physical and mental impairments that are chronic and severe and have occurred during the growth and developmental period of their lives. The most commonly known conditions that fall under the category of developmental disabilities are mental retardation, cerebral palsy, autism, epilepsy and Down syndrome.

Diabetes

Diabetes is a disease in which the body's ability to use carbohydrates (sugar) works improperly. The body of an individual who has diabetes is unable to burn up carbohydrates because of a lack of insulin, which is produced by the pancreas. The lack of insulin in the blood prevents the storage of glucose (the body's gasoline) in the cells of the liver. Consequently, blood sugar accumulates in the bloodstream in greater than usual amounts.

Signs of diabetes may include a general lack of energy, frequent urination, excessive thirst and a sudden loss of weight. There are two types of diabetes: the childhood type (Type I) in which inadequate insulin is made, and the adult type (Type II) in which the insulin does not work properly. Insulin shots are almost always required for the childhood type whereas the adult-type diabetics can help control the disease with a special diabetic diet, proper use of medication and participating in a vigorous aerobic exercise program at least three to four times per week. Diabetes became a part of the National Handicap Act because it is the leading cause of loss of vision and of new cases of kidney failure in adults ages 20 to 70 in the United States. Children under 20 rarely have these problems.

The major concern on the ski slopes is the occurrence of low blood sugar (hypoglycemia or insulin shock). The usual early symptoms are shakiness, hunger, sweating and weakness. If not treated early it can advance to confusion and eventually even loss of consciousness or a seizure. The early treatment is to give a source of sugar (two packets of sugar, juice, sugar-pop or candy). It takes 10 minutes for the blood sugar to return to normal. The person should rest during this 10 minutes and not return to skiing. Then, after the 10 minutes, a more substantial snack such as a granola bar or sandwich can be eaten. Never allow a person with diabetes to go off by himself if he has low blood sugar. The low blood sugar might cause confusion or loss of consciousness. People with diabetes do not want to be treated differently from other people. The ski program allows them to realize they can do activities others can do. Exercise, along with insulin, diet and the psyche, is one of the four important parameters of diabetes control, and skiing is a great exercise.

There are many long-term complications of diabetes that can occur even if the individual does all the things he should do to take care of himself. Diabetes is the most common cause of new blindness and renal failure in the U.S. Other complications include: heart attacks, strokes and gangrene (needing amputation). This is because every organ in the body is affected by the disease, usually due to blood vessel thickening, neuropathy (changes in the peripheral and autonomic nervous system) and retinopathy (progressive impairment of the circulation in the eyes).

Down Syndrome

Down syndrome is a combination of birth defects including mental retardation. The child with Down syndrome may have oval-shaped eyes, a tongue that seems big for the mouth and a short neck. The child or adult is usually short in stature and has unusual looseness of the joints.

The degree of mental retardation varies widely, from mild to moderate to severe. There is no way to predict the mental development of a child with Down syndrome from the physical appearance.

Many of those with Down syndrome have heart abnormalities and frequently surgery can correct these problems. A child with Down syndrome may have many colds, bronchitis and pneumonia. These children, like all others, should receive regular medical care including eye and hearing tests as well as regular immunizations.

A baby is formed when the egg from the mother and the sperm from the father come together. Normally, egg and sperm cells each have 23 chromosomes. Chromosomes are the hereditary information packets of every living cell. In the usual case of a child with Down syndrome, either the egg or the sperm cell contributes 24 chromosomes instead of 23. The result is that the chromosomes present total 47 instead of the normal 46. The extra chromosome causes the mental and physical characteristics of Down syndrome.

Epilepsy

Epilepsy is a physical condition that happens when there are sudden, brief changes in how the brain works. When brain cells are not working properly, a person's consciousness, movements or actions may be changed for a short time. These physical changes are called epileptic seizures. Epilepsy is therefore sometimes called a seizure disorder. Epilepsy affects people in all nations and of all races.

In about half of all cases no one cause can be found. Among the rest, epilepsy may be caused by any one of a number of things that make a difference in the way the brain works. For example, head injuries or lack of oxygen during birth may damage the delicate electrical system in the brain. Other causes include brain tumors, genetic conditions (such as tuberous sclerosis), lead poisoning, problems in development of the brain before birth and illnesses like meningitis, encephalitis or even severe cases of measles.

The brain is the control center for the body. Normal electrical signals between cells make the brain and body work correctly. The cells work like little switches, turning electrical charges on and off automatically. But sometimes it is as if some cells get stuck in the "on" position. The extra energy they produce affects other cells and spreads to other parts or through all of the brain. This extra energy blocks out our usual awareness of things around us, or may change the way the world looks, or may make our bodies move automatically. Sometimes it may cause a convulsion. These seizures usually last a short time (a matter of seconds or two to three minutes), and then end naturally as special chemicals in the brain bring cell activity back to normal.

Seizures can be of two major types—convulsive and nonconvulsive. A convulsive seizure (also called grand mal) happens when the whole brain is suddenly swamped with extra electrical energy. It often starts with a hoarse cry caused by air being suddenly forced out of the lungs. The person falls to the ground unconscious. The body stiffens briefly and then begins jerking movements.

Bladder or bowel control is sometimes lost. The tongue may be bitten. A frothy saliva may appear around the mouth caused by air being forced through mouth fluids. Breathing may get very shallow and even stop for a few moments. Sometimes the skin turns a bluish color because the lower rate of breathing is supplying less oxygen than usual. The jerking movements then slow down, and the seizure ends naturally after a minute or two. After returning to consciousness the person may feel confused and sleepy. In some cases only a very short recovery period is required, and most people can go back to their normal activities after resting for a while.

Fragile X Syndrome

Fragile X syndrome is a genetic condition that is identified by a weakness or break in the structure of the X chromosome. This can result in mental retardation or autism, which is characterized by extreme withdrawal or refusal to communicate. This is the leading cause of mental retardation, second only to Down syndrome, and is responsible for one out of 10 cases of autism.

Eighty percent of boys who inherit the syndrome will suffer mental impairment, ranging from severe retardation to a low to normal intelligence. Males have a higher risk of inheriting this condition because of their XY chromosome configuration. The XX chromosome (in females) hides some of the impairments.

Individuals with Fragile X syndrome may develop oversized or cupped ears, slightly elongated faces and enlarged testicles. The condition is linked with low to average intelligence in individuals with no physical abnormalities. Sometimes this condition is indicated by poor eye contact and certain hand mannerisms such as hand flapping and biting. Fragile X is linked with hyperactivity, violent outbursts, depression, coordination difficulties and learning disabilities, particularly in math.

Friedreich's Ataxia

Friedreich's ataxia is a genetic disorder resulting in progressive deterioration of the nervous system, causing an inability to coordinate voluntary muscle movement. Intelligence and the special senses are usually unimpaired.

The disorder usually begins between the ages of 10 and 13, starting with an unsteadiness in the legs. Over a period of eight to 10 years, the individual will lose the ability to walk unassisted. This condition is often associated with fatigue, total absence of tendon reflexes, weakness and loss of coordinated arm and hand movement resulting in difficulty with manipulative tasks. The individual is very dependent upon visual cues for motor function. It is known that the disorder is inherited. No cure has been developed for Friedreich's ataxia. Medical management is dictated by the individual's needs as they develop. Some individuals need to wear braces or use wheelchairs or other adaptive devices that will assist the individual in being independent. As the disorder progresses, deformities will occur, especially in the spinal column and feet. The individual will experience difficulty with speech. The heart muscle can also be affected.

Head Injury

See Traumatic Brain Injury.

Learning Disability

Persons who have a learning disability do not have mental retardation nor are they slow learners. Rather, these individuals usually have average or above-average intelligence. Additionally, there is usually no obvious physical disability, and this is why it is often referred to as a hidden disability.

An individual with a learning disability has difficulty with the messages to the brain becoming jumbled, thus making it difficult for the individual to learn in one or more of the academic areas. However, they can learn and be successful as lawyers, doctors, social service workers, etc. They must learn to compensate for their difficulties by learning in ways that are different from the average ways people learn.

As with many other disabilities, a variety of factors may be responsible for a person having a learning disability; these may include:
Prenatal—maternal malnutrition, toxemia in pregnancy, alcoholism during pregnancy, taking certain drugs, RH incompatibility, infectious viral illness in the pregnant mother.
During birth—long difficult delivery, lack of oxygen, prematurity, dry birth, intracranial pressure (due to forceps delivery), a narrow pelvic arch in the mother or too rapid delivery.
After birth—delay in breathing, high fever at an early age, sharp blow to the head from a fall or accident, lead poisoning, drug intoxication, suffocation or breath holding or severe nutritional deficiencies. Following are some of the most common characteristics of a learning disability. A person with a learning disability will not show all of the characteristics, and a person who does not have a learning disability may also show some of the characteristics:

- short attention span/easily distracted
- difficulty in following instructions
- poor reasoning ability
- inability to set realistic goals by themselves
- poor reading ability/adds, omits words when reading
- difficulty distinguishing between p, g, k, d and q
- reads "on" for "no," "was" for "saw," etc.
- difficulty with concepts of left, right, above, below, up, down, yesterday, tomorrow, in, out, etc.
- difficulty telling time
- difficulty writing/writes "41" for "14"
- poor hand-eye coordination
- clumsy/accident-prone
- disorganized/loses things
- quick-tempered/easily irritated
- impulsive/gets caught up in details
- childish and bossy behavior/needs constant recognition
- usually a loner

Meniere's Disease

Caused by	1. Too much fluid in the inner ear
	2. Excessive amount of inner ear infections or chronic inner ear infection
Symptoms	1. Constant ringing in the ear (usually only one ear is afflicted)
	2. Vertigo dizziness; usually long-lasting and severe episodes

	3. Loss of hearing in afflicted ear, although many people have a loss of hearing in the other ear due to a history of infections
Major drug used	Antivert (may cause drowsiness, balance problems)

Mental Retardation

By definition, a mentally retarded person is one who, from childhood, develops at a below-average rate and experiences difficulty in learning, social adjustment and economic productivity.

The vast majority are classified as mildly retarded. They differ from nonretarded people only in the rate and degree of intellectual development. In fact, their retardation is not usually apparent until they enter school. And then, as adults, they often lose their identity as retarded when they enter the job market and daily community life.

Moderately retarded persons usually show their developmental delay before they reach school age. However, appropriate community-based education throughout their developmental years can prepare these people to live a satisfying and productive life.

Severely and profoundly retarded persons show the most pronounced developmental problems and frequently have handicaps in addition to mental retardation. Systematic training efforts have proven that, with very few exceptions, severely and profoundly retarded persons can learn to tend to their basic needs. Many also can perform useful work activities, with supervision, and can otherwise adapt to normal patterns of life.

Any condition that hinders or interferes with intellectual development before or during birth or in the early childhood years can be the cause of mental retardation. And although more than 250 causes are known, these account for only one-fourth of all identified cases.

Among the well-known causes are: German measles in the mother during the first three months of pregnancy, syphilis, meningitis, toxoplasmosis, Rh-factor incompatibility between mother and infant, malnutrition and chromosome abnormalities, such as Down syndrome.

Undoubtedly, among the mildly retarded there are many whose development has been adversely affected by things like inadequate diet, poor prenatal care and lack of learning opportunities. Infants and young children need the right kind of mental activity just as they need the right kind of physical activity. And when this activity is lacking, delays can occur. So these early years, when the nervous system is maturing and language is developing, are very critical.

Destruction of brain tissue or interference with brain development in babies or small children frequently produces mental retardation. This accounts for a large number of cases of moderate, severe and profound mental retardation. We can't be sure to what degree brain damage contributes in cases of mild retardation, and expert opinion is divided.

**Multiple
Sclerosis**

Multiple sclerosis (MS) is a neurological disease affecting the brain and spinal cord of the central nervous system. The myelin sheath is the insulation around nerves that allows messages from the brain and spinal cord to be carried throughout the body. In MS some of the protective myelin gets destroyed and all messages are not carried out as they should be. This causes a variety of seemingly strange symptoms, which come and go over time, and vary depending on the location of the disruptions in the myelin. So no two people have the same set of symptoms, and the person with MS will have different symptoms at different times. MS is not fatal, and the majority of people with the disease are able to lead healthy and productive lives with some lifestyle changes.

The symptoms of MS vary widely, are unpredictable and are often "invisible." The most common are: chronic fatigue, heat sensitivity, balance problems, difficulty walking (gait disturbances), sensory complaints (numbness, feelings described as prickling, burning, constriction, tingling, electrical shock and different kinds of pain), loss of position sense (not knowing where a body part is in space), incoordination, tremors, spasticity (stiffness and/or bouncing leg, arm or body part[s]), bladder problems and visual problems (blurred, double, involuntary rapid eye movement, even blindness). In some severe cases partial or complete paralysis and mild cognitive impairment can occur. The cause and cure are unknown, although symptoms often can be managed with medications, exercise, stress management techniques, learning to balance rest and exercise to avoid excessive fatigue, well-balanced diet and avoidance of situations that increase body heat (heat can temporarily worsen symptoms for many people with MS). The majority of people with MS are diagnosed between the ages of 20 and 40. It is commonly found in colder climates and is not contagious or hereditary, although a genetic predisposition is suspected.

There are four different types of MS: (1) benign: mild or completely remitting attacks with long symptom-free periods (20 percent); (2) relapsing-remitting: periodic onset of symptoms followed by partial or complete recovery, with plateaus of stable involvement (25 percent); (3) relapsing-progressive: attacks with some recovery and significant residual involvement, with a slow deterioration of function (40 percent) and (4) chronic-progressive: continuous deterioration of function over years, or in rare cases, months (15 percent).

The majority of people with MS (about 70 percent) are mobile (do not use a wheelchair to get around) 30 years after diagnosis. Most people with MS have some symptoms at all times.

**Muscular
Dystrophy**

Muscular dystrophy (MD) is a group of at least nine diseases that are inherited and are characterized by progressive degeneration and weakness of voluntary muscles and skeletal muscles, which control movement. It is not considered fatal, although some of the diseases shorten the normal life span. Five of the nine main types of MD have their onset during adulthood. Each of the different diseases differs in severity, muscles most often affected, age of onset and how fast the disease progresses. It is more common in males than females. MD is caused by a defective gene, which is the body's basic unit of heredity, passed from parent to child.

The most common MD is Myotonic MD, which usually starts between the ages of 20 and 40, has a very slow progression and affects the central nervous system, eyes, heart and endocrine glands. Muscle weakness progresses slowly and symptoms vary even in the same families. Duchenne MD is the second most common, and the most common and severe childhood form of MD. The age of onset is usually between two and six years. This is the only form of the disease that can become fatal, usually in the 20s. In this form fat and connective tissue replace muscle. Most children need a wheelchair by 12 years. The cause of rapid deterioration is when breathing problems become more severe, leading to an early death. Becker MD is third in incidence, and usually starts between the ages of two and 16, even up to 25. It is similar to Duchenne, except the progression is slower, and its severity varies. There is a much longer life expectancy as well. Limb-Girdle MD is the fourth most common form of MD, and starts in late childhood to middle age. The progression is usually slow, and life span can be shortened. This disease affects the shoulders, girdle and pelvic girdle, causing progressive weakness. Most people are able to walk for many years after onset. Faciocapulohumeral MD is the fifth most common, and begins in the teens to early adulthood. It affects the face, the shoulders and the girdle. It progresses slowly, with long remissions interspersed with short periods of rapid muscle deterioration and weakness. In most cases its course is mild, but can impair the ability to walk. Congenital MD is sixth in incidence, and as it sounds it begins at birth. It causes generalized muscle weakness, joint deformities and progresses slowly to no progression at all. Oculopharyngeal MD is the seventh most common form of MD, and the age of onset is between 40 and 70. Its progression is slow, and it mostly limits itself to the muscles of the eyes and throat, including difficulty in swallowing. In late stages it sometimes causes weakness of the pelvic and shoulder muscles. Distal MD is eighth in incidence. It usually shows itself between 40 and 60 years, and primarily affects the hands. Its progression is slow. It may progress to affecting the feet, lower arms and legs. It does not usually affect the life span. Emery-Dreifuss MD is the most rare form of MD. It begins in childhood to early teens. It causes shortening of the elbow, knee and ankle muscles and an abnormal heart rhythm, which can be regulated with a pacemaker. It progresses slowly, and life span is unaffected so long as the heart problems are treated.

MD is treated with physical and occupational therapies, exercise programs, use of adaptive aids and surgery for muscle shortening. Lifestyle changes need to be made depending on the extent of the disability and involvement.

Myasthenia Gravis

Myasthenia gravis (MG) is a neuromuscular disease that affects transmission of messages to the voluntary muscles (skeletal muscles and muscles normally under our own command) of the body. It is most common in women 20 to 40 years old and men over the age of 55. It is considered to be an autoimmune disease, meaning that the body's immune system attacks itself. In this case it attacks acetylcholine receptors, which control neuromuscular transmission. This interferes with the nerve impulses from the nerves to the muscles, and causes excessive fatiguability of muscle function.

The symptoms may include any combination of the following: abnormal and severe muscle weakness of any muscle group, fatigue, double vision, difficulty swallowing including choking on food and aspiration (where the food goes into the lungs), difficulty speaking, drooping of one or both eyelids and facial muscle weakness that resembles a sleepy type of look. Vigorous exercise, excessive heat and cold, infections, surgery or trauma can worsen the disease and even lead to a life-threatening crisis. A myasthenia crisis can interfere with breathing and requires immediate hospitalization.

The primary treatment is to give anticholinesterase drugs (such as pyridostigmine), which increases the time that acetylcholine is available. In many cases surgery—removal of the thymus gland—improves the disease and can cause an immediate remission. Most people have the surgery in combination with the use of medications. Of most benefit to the person with the disease is to know as much about the disease and medications as possible, and to make the appropriate lifestyle changes to avoid a crisis. Balancing rest and activity and stress management techniques are useful as well as using appropriate adaptive aids and self-help devices to aid weakened muscles. Other treatments that might be used in MG are: immunosuppressive medications (like steroids or cytoxin) and sometimes plasma exchanges.

Parkinson's Disease

Parkinson's disease (PD) is a central nervous system disease that is chronic, degenerative and progressive. For years it has been thought to be a disease of old age, affecting most people after the age of 50. However, an increasing number of young people develop PD in their 20s to 40s, possibly because it is now more easily recognized, or the incidence may be on the increase. It seems to affect men slightly more than women (six out of 10 cases). The disease affects the young in different ways than the old. Young people tend to have greater tremors, but their balance and walking are better. They may have more involuntary movement, but their thinking ability seems to be less affected. Also, their disease seems to develop at a slower pace.

The main symptoms of PD are: tremor, rigidity, complete or partial loss of muscle movement and loss of reflexes that help maintain normal posture. The tremor is more active at rest, and can disappear during movement, while it is absent in sleep. Rigidity is seen as stiffness, aching and tightness and slows movement. The change in muscle movement makes it hard for the person to initiate movement, like getting up from a chair or starting to walk. The postural changes affect balance and cause difficulty in maintaining an upright position, making the head fall forward.

There is no cure for PD. The cause is unknown, but it is thought to be from a chemical imbalance in the brain, primarily a problem with utilization of dopamine. It is managed by the medication Levodopa (which turns into dopamine in the brain) by itself or in combination with Sinemet (which helps prevent the destruction of Levodopa), along with physical therapy. People with PD are encouraged to keep as physically active as possible and have an active exercise program to keep muscles limber. Outdoor exercise such as walking is of great benefit. When walking and initiation of movement are a problem, rocking back on the heels and raising the toes helps start movement. Getting up from a seated position often takes time and is helped by rocking back and forth, bending at the waist and pushing up with the arms.

Polyradiculitis (Guillain-Barré Syndrome)

Polyradiculitis is a disease of the peripheral nervous system (all of the nervous system except the brain and the spinal cord) and the cranial nerves. It causes muscle weakness to partial or total paralysis. It is a life-threatening disease since paralysis may progress rapidly, ascending from the feet through the face and causing respiratory failure (inability to breathe).

The symptoms may include any or all of the following: muscle weakness, numbness and tingling, difficulty chewing and swallowing, difficulty breathing, heart arrhythmias, urinary retention, paralysis. Often there is an initial severe attack with a very long recovery period. Many people are left with residual symptoms and symptom-related disability and chronic fatigue. Some people have more than one attack of the severe life-threatening symptoms.

Post Polio

Poliomyelitis (polio) is a viral disease that is contagious through the gastrointestinal system (saliva, feces and vomit). It was widespread throughout the world until the vaccine (Live Oral Trivalent Poliovirus Vaccine) was developed and distributed in the 1950s. However, it is endemic throughout the world, and epidemics still occur. Nonimmunized people, especially children, immunosuppessed people, pregnant women and people who have had recent tonsillectomies and tooth extractions are most susceptible to the disease. Some people have contracted the disease from the live vaccine. There are three types, but the most severe affects the central nervous system and causes paralysis. The paralysis may be confined to a small group of muscles, or may be more widespread including respiratory muscles.

In order to understand the needs of the person with post polio, it is important to understand the initial course of the disease and the types of medical and surgical interventions that were used. It is perplexing, because we think of a disease as a onetime event, and many people with post polio look perfectly "normal." After the initial infection, if any paralysis was present, the residual effects last a lifetime. Many people have had numerous reconstructive surgeries of various limbs and the spine. Some of the residual disability is visible, like having one leg or arm shorter than the other. What isn't understood is that there is often residual respiratory and trunk instability, causing balance problems, fatiguability, and shortness of breath with physical exertion. Most people have several groups of muscles that are weak and easily fatigued. Since circulation may still be impaired, limbs can be affected by excessive cold, often without the individual's awareness. Care should be taken to prevent frostbite.

Some post polio people develop what has been called post polio syndrome. It is a progressive, degenerative disease that can be both neuromuscular and orthopedic (affecting the bone and spine) in nature. It is characterized by excessive fatigue and numerous other symptoms, which vary from person to person. Some of the possible symptoms are: nerve damage resulting in muscle weakness, muscle atrophy (shrinking) and muscle spasms, carpal tunnel syndrome, disc disease (the pads between the vertebrae of the spine get damaged), scoliosis (curvature of the spine), other forms of degeneration of the spine, swallowing disorders and other symptoms. This disorder is very disabling since the resulting problems are added to the prexisting disability present since the onset of the initial polio infection. There is no cure. People are treated according to symptoms. Some options are: physical and occupational therapies, exercise programs, learning how to balance rest and activity, use of adaptive devices and corrective surgeries.

Reflex Sympathetic Dystrophy Syndrome

Reflex sympathetic dystrophy syndrome (RSDS) is thought to be an automatic action (reflex) caused by a disorder of the sympathetic nervous system (SNS), a part of the autonomic nervous system (the part of the nervous system that is in control of involuntary functions). The SNS is located alongside the spinal cord and controls the opening up and closing down of blood vessels and sweat glands. In RSDS it appears that this function is slowed down or damaged. This causes irregular blood supply to the areas that are affected—usually one or more extremities, but may be any area of the body. RSDS is a disabling multi-symptom disease with simultaneous involvement of skin, nerves, muscles, blood vessels, and bones. There are many symptoms, but the most common and pronounced symptom is pain. The pain is described as burning, severe and constant. There is often swelling in the areas involved, muscle spasm and limitation of motion and use. The blood supply changes along with nerve involvement cause "Raynaud's phenomenon," where the area turns blue, white and red. This is dangerous in the cold because the person is very susceptible to frostbite, so precautions should be taken to prevent overcooling of the affected parts.

Other symptoms include osteoporosis (softening of the bones); joint tenderness and swelling; skin tissue atrophy (shrinking) with dryness, scaling and nail changes; atrophy and weakness of the muscles. In later stages the pain becomes intractable, and flexor tendon contractures can occur.

The cause and cure are unknown, but a number of precipitating factors have been identified such as trauma, heart disease, spinal cord disorders, surgery, infections and/or cerebral lesions. Both men and women are affected, but the incidence is slightly higher in females. Most people are diagnosed after 50, but children and young adults can also develop this disorder. It is treated by medications for pain management, muscle relaxants, steroids and antiinflammatories. Other treatments include: physical therapy, nerve blocks, surgery and transcutaneous electrical stimulation (TENS).

Spina Bifida

Spina bifida (also called myelomeningocele or meningomyelocele) is a birth defect of the spinal column and spinal cord. The defect occurs in the fetus in early pregnancy when the covering over the spinal cord forms a "sac-like pouch" and the vertebra(e) do(es) not completely form to enclose the spinal cord at the defect site. Nerves from the spinal cord may grow into this sac like pouch and affect the connection between the brain and the spinal cord and the area the spinal cord innervates. Different muscles are controlled by nerves that connect to the spinal cord at different levels. The amount of nerve involvement varies greatly from individual to individual, depending on deficit level. Although the defect most often is in the lower spine, it can occur at higher levels. The lower the level, the fewer number of nerves involved and therefore, the more lower-extremity function the individual will have. In some cases, not all of the nerves at a given level of the defect are affected. In these cases, the individual may have "spotty" muscle function from nerves originating below the defect site.

In higher defects, the individual often cannot walk due to paralysis of the lower extremities and poor muscle control of the trunk. These individuals may be confined to wheelchairs for mobility. In very low-level defects, individuals may be able to walk without or with minimal bracing. A wide variety of function and bracing needs are noted between these extremes of defect levels. Bracing can provide the stability needed to allow the individual to stand when muscle power is unbalanced or weak. Muscle imbalances often contribute to deformities of the bones and joints of the lower extremities and the spine.

The spinal cord includes nervous tissue relating to touch, temperature, pain and pressure as well as muscle function. Therefore, these sensations may also be affected in areas innervated from or below the defect site. The amount of deficit is also affected by the amount of spinal cord that is actually damaged at the defect site. Skin problems can lead to infection and can often be slow to heal. Therefore,

Syndrome

1. A group of signs and symptoms that occur together and characterize a particular abnormality.
2. A set of concurrent things (emotions or actions) that usually form an identifiable pattern.

Larry Kunz, spina bifida, four track racer and national champion.　PHOTO: STEVE STONE

it is very important to take measures to protect the skin from problems such as increased pressure, pressure areas, frostbite. excessive heat or cold, etc. Swelling or edema in the lower extremities is often noted in spina bifida because of poor circulation. Thus, pressure areas from shoes and braces are of concern. Visual skin checks are of utmost importance in order to maintain healthy skin. Spinal fluid normally passes between (1) small blood vessels around the brain, (2) the spinal canal (in the center of the spinal cord) and (3) the ventricles in the center of the brain. Often the balance between the absorption of this fluid by the blood vessels is affected by the spinal defect of the spina bifida individual. If this occurs, it is called hydrocephalus. This creates increased spinal fluid pressure on the brain and brain damage could occur. In order to treat increased pressure caused by hydrocephalus, a shunting mechanism can be surgically implanted between the brain and the abdomen or heart where the fluid can be reabsorbed. The shunting mechanism is often identified by a prominence under the skin behind the ear and the prominence of a small tube running under the surface of the skin down the side of the neck and across the chest. Care must be taken to prevent direct blows to the side of the head where the shunt is located.

Nerves that control voluntary urination and defecation come from the lower portion of the spinal cord. This control is often affected in the individual with myelomeningocele. Urinary control by means of manual emptying of the bladder by pressure on the abdomen (Crede method) or use of a catheter to collect or create voiding may be used. A regular voiding program is necessary to prevent bladder and kidney infections as well as excessive back pressure on the kidneys. Bowels are usually managed through careful diets and when necessary, manual stimulation of the muscles controlling voiding and/or medication. Unexpected bladder or bowel voiding has been noted on occasion with increased physical activity or other forms of stimulation.

Many spina bifida individuals who do not walk or place very little stress on the lower extremities, as with standing, develop weakened bony structures that are more susceptible to fracture. This is particularly true in the long bones of the lower extremities and caution should be taken accordingly.

It is especially important to note that many spina bifida individuals, as well as those with other neurological problems, have learning problems and require special consideration. Evaluation of the individual's learning style and using this as a guideline in working with him are essential.

In conclusion, the individual with spina bifida has a complexity of characteristics. An understanding of his abilities and knowledge of the special precautions that must be taken are very important for those working with individuals who have spina bifida.

Spinal Cord Injury

In the United States, over 150,000 people have spinal cord injury (SCI). The incidence is 25 to 35 new cases per 100,000 people annually. Recent data from the Spinal Cord Injury National Data Bank in Phoenix, Arizona, covering 3,123 SCI patients, reveal the following causes of injury: 36 percent, motor vehicle accidents; 16 percent, falls; 13 percent, gunshot wounds; 10 percent, diving; 6 percent, motorcycle accidents; 5 percent, falling objects and the remaining percentages divided into various other causes including sporting activities, medical/surgical complications and stab wounds. Snow skiing accounts for only .26 percent of the injuries.

Of these patients, 82 percent are male and 18 percent female. The age distribution is as follows: 0–14 years, 5 percent; 15–29 years, 62 percent; 30–44 years, 20 percent; 45–59 years, 10 percent; and greater than 60 years, 3 percent.

From these data, it can be seen that the majority of persons with SCI are young, active males, often interested in continuing an active lifestyle after their SCI. One of these active endeavors is skiing.

The central nervous system (CNS) is composed of the brain, spinal cord and spinal nerves (Fig. 1). The spinal cord is an extension of the brain and is a cylindrical structure composed of nerve cells and fibers. Spinal nerves arise from the spinal cord and connect your brain with your muscles, skin and internal organs. When the CNS is intact, it is an extremely efficient communication system between brain and muscles, etc. The spinal cord sits in between these two areas, acting much like a telephone line and communicating two-way messages. Emanating from the spinal cord, 31 pairs of spinal nerves branch out and connect to all parts of the body at various levels. Spinal nerves from the upper part of the cord connect with the upper part of the torso, arms and hands. Spinal nerves from the lower part of the cord connect with lower torso, pelvis, thighs, calves and feet. Branching and dividing even further from the spinal cord are the peripheral nerves that reach every millimeter of your skin surface, every muscle, every blood vessel and every bone.

How the Nervous System Works

Muscle movement begins in the brain and electrical impulses descend through the lateral and anterior parts of the spinal cord, to the spinal nerves and out to the muscles. This is termed the motor pathway. When this pathway is injured, the result is paralysis or the inability to move muscles. Sensation occurs when impulses travel from the skin or organs through the spinal nerves and ascend up the posterior and anterior/lateral parts of the spinal cord to the brain. This is termed the sensory pathway. When this pathway is injured, the result is loss of sensation. The type of motor/sensory loss a person with SCI has depends on what areas of the spinal cord were damaged.

Anatomy

The spinal cord is protected by multiple bony structures called vertebrae, which compose the spinal column commonly known as the "back bone." The spinal canal runs through the center of these vertebrae, and the spinal cord is located in this canal (Fig. 2).

Figure 1

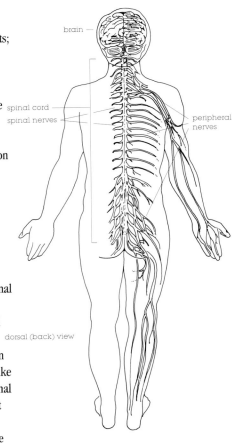

brain

spinal cord

spinal nerves

peripheral nerves

dorsal (back) view

Figure 2

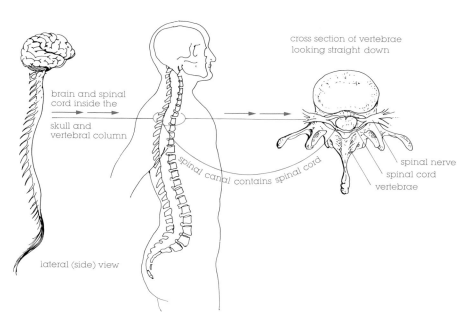

cross section of vertebrae
looking straight down

brain and spinal
cord inside the

skull and
vertebral column

spinal canal contains spinal cord

spinal nerve
spinal cord
vertebrae

lateral (side) view

What Happens After SCI

There are four major divisions of the spinal column (Figure 3 on page 154):
1. The cervical region, or neck
2. The thoracic region, or chest
3. The lumbar region. or lower back
4. The sacral region, or tail bone

The cervical region contains the first seven vertebrae and the first eight spinal nerves. The thoracic region is composed of the next 12 vertebrae and the next 12 spinal nerves. The next five vertebrae and spinal nerves make up the lumbar region. The last section of the spinal column is the sacrum and coccyx. Here nine vertebrae fuse together into two separate bone structures. This area contains six spinal nerves.

If a spinal cord injury occurs in the cervical region, the diagnosis is quadriplegia or weakness of all four extremities. If the injury occurs in other regions, the diagnosis is paraplegia or weakness of the two lower extremities.

The spinal cord can be injured at any area along its length (usually by a broken bone of the vertebrae or dislocation of spinal nerves of the vertebrae). In general, the higher the level of injury, the greater the loss of function. The parts and functions of the body that are located above the point of injury will continue to function unimpaired. The parts and functions that are below the point of injury, how-ever, cannot function in their normal way. Messages from above and below the level of injury are blocked by the damage to the spinal cord and can no longer reach their destination for an appropriate response.

Classification of Injury

Damage to the spinal cord can result in either a complete or an incomplete injury. A complete injury results in total loss of motor and sensory function below the level of injury. This implies damage across the entire level of the spinal cord, affecting both the motor and sensory pathways. An incomplete injury results in partial loss of motor and sensory function below the level of injury.

A person has the description of quadriplegia/quadriparesis if damage has occurred in the cervical spinal cord area, resulting in total (plegia) or partial (paresis) loss of motor function in the upper extremities. Paraplegia/paraparesis occurs from damage to the thoracic, lumbar or sacral areas of the spinal cord, resulting in total or partial loss of lower extremity motor function.

Level of Injury

A complete quadriplegia has intact motor and sensory function at the C-6 spinal segment and above, with all segments below C-6 lost and without motor/sensory functioning. An incomplete C-6 injury has intact motor and sensory function at the C-6 spinal segment and above with partial preservation of motor/sensory function below the C-6 level.

The most common levels of injury are C5–6, T6–7 and T12–L1. Approximately 50 percent of SCI persons are quadriplegic/quadriparetic and 50 percent are paraplegia/paraparetic. (See Figs. 4 and 5 for motor and sensory distribution of spinal nerve.)

Figure 3

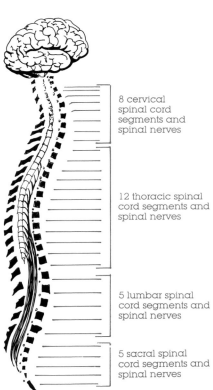

8 cervical
spinal cord
segments and
spinal nerves

12 thoracic spinal
cord segments and
spinal nerves

5 lumbar spinal
cord segments and
spinal nerves

5 sacral spinal
cord segments and
spinal nerves

Figure 4   Figure 5

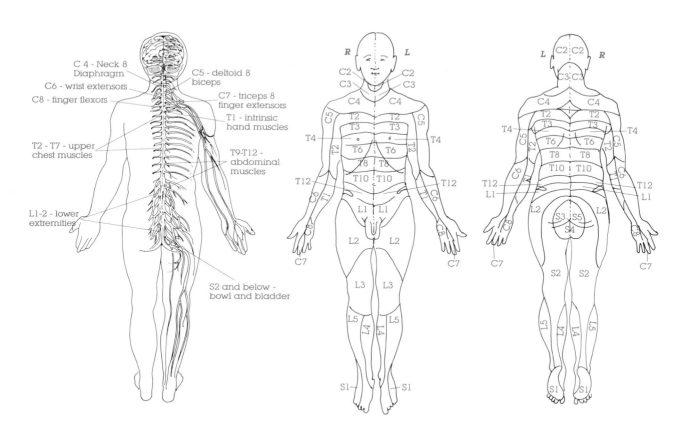

Functional Levels of Independence in Skiing

L4–5 S-1 Injury: Loss of sensation at the appropriate level, paralysis/paresis of hip extensors, knee flexors and ankle plantar/dorsiflexors. These people are usually ambulators requiring ankle-foot bracing and forearm crutches or canes. As skiers, these people stand up with support provided by the rigid ski boots and outrigger-type ski poles.

L2–3 Injury: Level of sensation moves higher up the body, paralysis/paresis as above with additional involvement of hip flexors and quadriceps or knee extensors; hip adductors may be weak. People often require knee-ankle-foot braces to stabilize the knee and ankle and a pair of forearm or axillary crutches for independent ambulation. A skier requires rigid boots, knee brace and outrigger poles. Many people with this level of injury are sit skiers or mono skiers.

T7–T12 Injury: Higher level of sensory loss, paralysis/paresis now includes the muscles of the lower back and abdomen. Trunk balance is compromised. Occasionally the person may ambulate with knee-ankle-foot braces and a walker. More commonly the person prefers a wheelchair for independent mobility. The skier is usually a sit skier or mono skier who functions very well with fair to good trunk balance and good upper extremity strength allowing the use of handheld "pick"-type ski poles for turning and control.

T1–T6 Injury: This level of injury now involves the upper chest muscles, which further compromises trunk balance. Locomotion is essentially limited to a wheelchair. The decreased trunk balance slightly limits independent wheelchair mobility because of an inability to perform "wheelies" that permit movement over curbs and other raised obstacles.

C8–T1 Injury: These people are quadriplegic/quadriparetic depending on the completeness of injury. Hand function is impaired with a decreased ability to flex the fingers and squeeze the hand into a fist.

C6–C7 Injury: At this level of injury the person has all the above deficits plus weakness of the finger extensors, wrist flexors/extensors, elbow extensors (tricep muscle) and partial weakness of the elbow flexors (bicep muscle). This upper-extremity weakness causes a decreased ability to functionally propel a manual wheelchair.

C5–C6 Injury: At this level of injury the person has weakness of the shoulder muscles (deltoids), further decreasing the ability to use the upper extremities in a functional way. A powered wheelchair is required for independent locomotion.

SCI Skier Special Considerations

C4–C5 Injury and Above: People with this level of injury have no real function except for some head and neck motion. See the C6–C7 injury description above. The sit skier is unable to perform functional arm ski maneuvers and goes along for a ride.

Thermoregulation—Impairment in internal temperature control may be seen in persons with spinal cord lesions above T8 and particularly at the cervical level. Adjustment to cooler ambient temperature is low, inconsistent and aided by the amount of cover over the person. This usually does not present a problem for the sit skier, bi skier or mono skier who is dressed appropriately. On very cold days the time out on the ski hill should be limited to approximately two to three hours with constant checks of the distal extremities. It must be remembered that as a sit skier, the person is sitting close to the snow and usually performing less work, which causes them to feel cold more quickly.

Spasticity—This is manifested by involuntary movements of muscles below the level of the SCI. These movements are due to exaggerated stretch reflex activity that occurs in the healthy portion of the spinal cord below the level of injury. The reflexes are exaggerated because the normal controlling messages from the brain are interrupted by the SCI. For example, if the legs are positioned in a way that stretches muscles, reflex muscle contractions can occur and appear as "flapping-like" movements. This reflex activity can be quite uncomfortable for the SCI person. To stop it, simply reposition the leg to reduce the stretch on the affected muscles.

Rick Ruscio, member of U.S. Disabled Ski Team. PHOTO: JEANNE SMITH

Skin—Sores can easily develop in areas of insensitive skin caused by prolonged pressure over bony prominence areas: ankles, knees, hips, sacrum and ischium (butt bone). All SCI persons have been taught the absolute necessity of avoiding prolonged pressure on the skin by performing weight shifts every few minutes. During sit skiing or mono skiing activity, the following rules should be observed: (1) Beware of improper positioning. A shearing force causes greater skin breakdown than a vertical force. (2) Check for areas of increased pressure/pinching. Provide adequate padding, below the heels, between the ankles and knees and under the buttocks. (3) Check that the sit ski, bi ski or monoski safety belts are straight and not twisted, which leads to increased pressure. (4) The quadriplegic person may need help in weight repositioning approximately every 30 minutes.

Bladder Functioning—An SCI can cause a number of control problems in bladder functioning. Each person has an individual program that involves regular emptying of the bladder. Some people have an indwelling catheter (tube) inserted into their bladder. Attached to the other end of the tube is a plastic bag that attaches to a leg and collects urine. This "leg bag" requires emptying when full to prevent urine backup and bladder distention. The SCI person has been well trained regarding bladder care. The sit skier, bi skier or mono skier needs to properly position his "leg bag" to prevent pressure on the bag or kinks in the tubing, which can cause urine backup. If a catheter loosens and leaks while skiing, it's important to stop skiing and perform all needed care.

Linda Spies, spioncerebellar degeneration.

Autonomic Dysreflexia—(Considered an emergency situation.) This condition occurs in persons with a spinal injury usually above the T6 level. It is a hypertensive (high blood pressure) crisis where the SCI person experiences severe sweating, goose bumps, flushed feeling, chilling without fever, severe pounding headache, high blood pressure and increased spasticity. The causes are mainly the problems mentioned above and include: bladder distention from a kinked indwelling catheter or full "leg bag," catheter irritation, skin pressure sores or spasticity from a stretched muscle. If autonomic dysreflexia occurs while sit skiing, bi skiing or mono skiing, the instructor/tetherer should do the following: (1) Set the person upright in the sit ski, bi ski or mono-ski to relieve shearing pressure on the skin. (2) Aid the person in checking the urinary catheter/leg bag for kinks or plugs, if requested, or if the person is physically unable to do this. (3) Check for spasticity and if noted, decrease the stretch on spastic muscles. (4) If symptoms continue, get the sit skier down the hill and to the first aid office immediately.

This is an emergency situation and if not managed correctly, could lead to stroke, coma and death. Fortunately, most SCI persons with optimal skin/bowel/bladder care will never develop this problem. Those who have experienced it know the symptoms and can tell you when it's occurring.

Summary: The majority of all SCI persons are young adults who were physically active prior to their injury and since their injury continue to desire athletic challenges. Skiing is one of the most adaptable sports for people with disabilities and can offer enjoyment, challenge and a sense of accomplishment. As with most other sporting activities, skiing has certain inherent risks that are partly responsible for the enjoyment experienced. These risks must be minimized, especially in the handicapped population. These people have already experienced a traumatic injury with some loss of physical functioning, and the last thing they need is another injury resulting in further hospitalization and loss of function. Providing the safest experience possible requires understanding what SCI is, knowing the different levels of injury and the resulting functional capabilities and knowing the special problems that can be experienced by an SCI person on the ski slope. If all these considerations have been dealt with before the sit skier gets up on the ski slope, unnecessary risk will be minimized, allowing for a safe, quality ski day.

Tom Balazy M.D.
Craig Hospital, Denver, Colorado.

Systematic Lupus Erythematosis

Systematic lupus erythematosis (usually just referred to as "lupus") is an autoimmune collagen vascular disease. Autoimmune means that the person's defense system attacks its own tissues as if they were foreign, like an invading virus. Collagen is the protein that is the main part of connective tissue (the tissue that holds all the tissues of our bodies together). And vascular refers to the blood vessels. In lupus, the body attacks connective tissue that causes inflammation and damage to many different parts of the entire body's blood vessels, skin surfaces, mucus membranes (found inside our mouths, and all passages and cavities that connect with the air) and other connective tissue.

Because of its widespread involvement, there is hardly a part of the body that does not have the potential of being affected. The main areas are: the skin, joints, muscles, kidneys, lungs, heart, brain and spinal cord. Not every person with lupus will have all the symptoms, and the symptoms will vary in each individual from day to day. People with lupus can have periods of severe illness, intermixed with periods of no illness and freedom from most or all symptoms. The symptoms come and go unpredictably, and no two people will seem the same.

The symptoms of lupus vary widely, are unpredictable and like MS are often "invisible." The general symptoms are aching, weakness, fatigue, fever and chills. Each body part it affects will have different symptoms. **skin:** rash, sun-sensitivity, hair loss, sores in the nose and mouth; **muscular-skeletal:** arthritis, swelling of the hands, muscle pain; **lungs:** inflammation of the lung lining (pleuritis), shortness of breath; **heart:** fluid in the aericardial sac (pericarditis), chest pain; **gastro-intestinal tract:** nausea, diarrhea, vomiting, constipation, severe abdominal pain; **lymph nodes:** enlarged, nodes, enlarged spleen and liver, or anemia, a low white blood cell or low platelet count; **central nervous system:** seizures, photosensitivity; **kidney:** kidney damage.

The cause and cure are unknown, although symptoms often can be managed with medication (like aspirin and steroids), use of sunscreens and avoiding sun exposure, rest (12 hours a day), learning to balance rest and activity, avoiding excessive fatigue, pain control, monitoring body temperature, counselling for both the individual and family, well-balanced diet and other stress management techniques. Care of fingers and toes is important for those affected by circulation problems (Raynaud's disease). The majority of people with lupus are women who are diagnosed between the ages of 20 and 30, 20 and 39 for men and between 4 and 18 in children.

Traumatic Brain Injury

Traumatic brain injury (TBI) is any injury to the head that disturbs or damages brain function, caused by many things including accidents, weapons and falls. Recent advances in medicine and technology have made surviving traumatic brain injury possible. In order to understand the effects of traumatic brain injury, it is important to understand what the brain does. It controls everything we do and who we are.

Activity	Brain Function
Physical functions	movements (walking, hand control, balance, coordination, breathing, heart rate, blood pressure
Communications	speaking, understanding, reading, writing
Thought processes	memory, problem-solving, making decisions
Interpreting senses	helping us understand what we see, feel, hear, taste and smell
Emotions	happiness, anger, sadness, fear, etc.

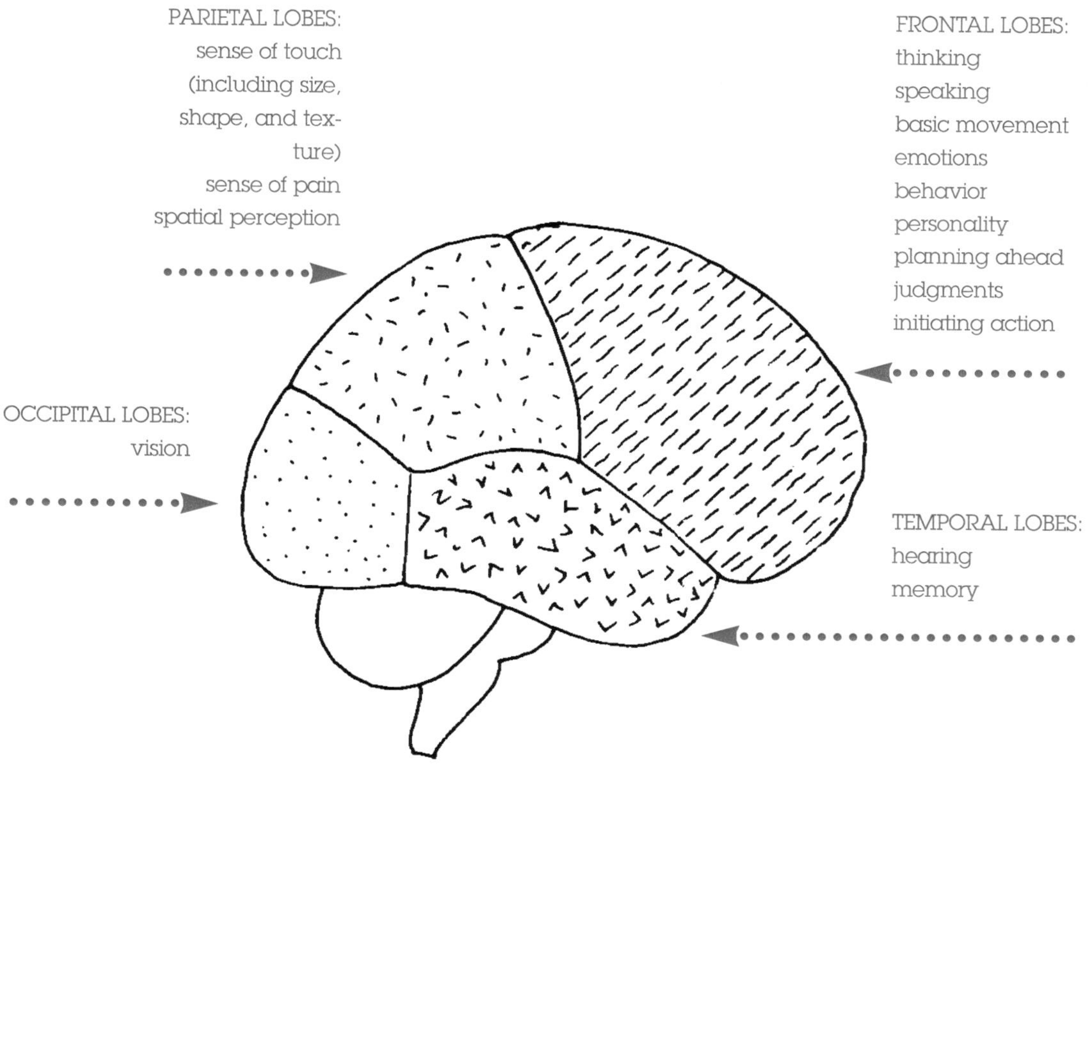

PARIETAL LOBES:
sense of touch
(including size,
shape, and tex-
ture)
sense of pain
spatial perception

FRONTAL LOBES:
thinking
speaking
basic movement
emotions
behavior
personality
planning ahead
judgments
initiating action

OCCIPITAL LOBES:
vision

TEMPORAL LOBES:
hearing
memory

Diffuse head injury is widespread microscopic damage throughout the brain. It is caused by *closed head injury*, which is trauma to the head that usually does not fracture the skull. Closed head injury occurs most frequently from auto or motorcycle accidents and from falls. With the violent impact of the accident, the head twists on the neck, causing the brain to twist or rotate in the skull, since the brain is not attached to the skull. Inside the brain, this rapid rotation stretches and tears neurons and their connections. Because of the tearing, microscopic areas of bleeding and damage occur throughout the entire brain, producing diffuse injury.

Closed head injury produces more damage to the deep, inner parts of the brain. If the cerebellum and brainstem connections are damaged, muscle coordination and balance can be affected.

Loss of consciousness occurs when deeper structures of the brain–those responsible for keeping us awake and alert–are injured by the rotational forces of closed head injury. Prolonged loss of consciousness is called coma. Coma is defined as when a person does not obey commands, utter words or open his eyes. Any closed head injury that produces a coma lasting over six hours is considered a severe injury. Usually, severely injured people will have problems with most brain functions—movement, sensation, memory, communication, thinking processes and behavior. The degree of seriousness and the permanence of these problems vary from patient to patient.

Because diffuse head injury affects neurons and their connections throughout the brain, the injured person can have problems with physical, emotional, thinking and behavioral areas—paying attention, reasoning and using good judgment. Memory problems are very common. Many head injured people need to be closely supervised for their safety. Often a person with traumatic brain injury can accomplish a given task, but may not be able to do it at the same level of quality as an uninjured person; or can complete the task successfully, but very slowly. Some of the most difficult problems are behavioral. These can include impulsive acts, irritability or depression, inappropriate behavior in public, physical or verbal outbursts and inappropriate responses to familiar people.

Focal injury can be caused in many ways, including gunshot or knife wounds or blows to the head that are hard enough to force pieces of the skull into the brain. Focal injury can also occur even if the skull is not fractured. A person can also receive focal injury during a closed head injury. This happens when the brain is torn by rough bones as it slides inside the skull, and bleeding occurs in these areas. In a car accident, other focal injury can result from what is called coup/contrecoup, which is French for "blow/opposite blow." Coup occurs when the brain hits the inside of the skull as the head strikes a solid object, like the dashboard. Contrecoup happens when the brain rebounds and hits the opposite side of the skull. Coup/contrecoup produces bruising and bleeding in both these areas of impact. Focal injury can also be caused by nontraumatic conditions such as strokes, brain tumors and ruptured blood vessels. In these cases, blood vessels become blocked or damaged, and neurons don't receive the oxygen they need.

Because areas of focal damage are specific, the problems that result are somewhat predictable. The left hemisphere of the brain controls the right side of the body, and the right hemisphere controls the left side of the body. Each hemisphere is also responsible for certain thinking and communication functions. If injury

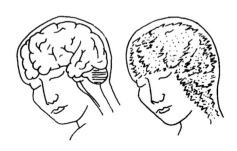

With a violent impact the head twists on neck, the brain twists and rotates in the skull

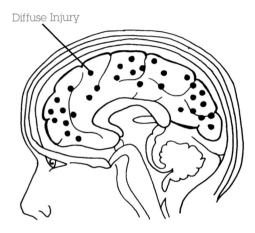

Diffuse Injury

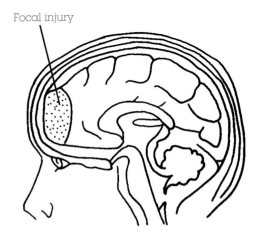

Focal injury

Coup

Contrecoup

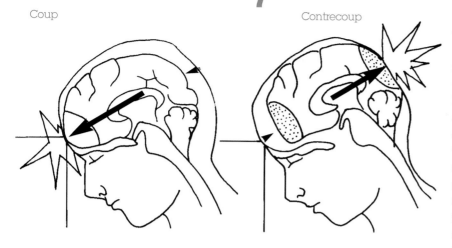

occurs on the left side of the brain, there will be some paralysis or loss of muscle. Other problems can develop, such as difficulty with spatial orientation and the ability to judge distance, shapes and form. If the brainstem is injured, vital activities can be impaired–breathing, heart rate and blood pressure. This causes a life-threatening situation. Brainstem injury also affects the ability to stay awake, to swallow, to move the eyes and to speak. It may also affect movement and control of the arms and legs. As the injured person comes out of coma and begins to recover, focal injury to specific parts of the brain may become more obvious.

Hypoxia is an injury to the brain caused by the lack of oxygen to the brain. Hypoxia can result from a heart attack, carbon monoxide poisoning near-drowning, among other causes. Hypoxia causes damage in specific areas of the brain. The problems that result from hypoxia are different for each person because the damage is different in each case. Certain areas of the brain are more sensitive to lack of oxygen. These may suffer more damage. People with hypoxia can have problems with many brain functions–movement, sensation, memory, communication, thinking processes and behavior. In this way the consequences of hypoxia can be similar to a combination of focal and diffuse injuries.

Left Hemiplegia–The patient referred to as a left hemiplegic or left hemi has experienced damage to the right hemisphere (right side) of his brain. The patient's left arm and/or leg may be paralyzed or weakened. There may also be paralysis or weakness of the left facial muscles.

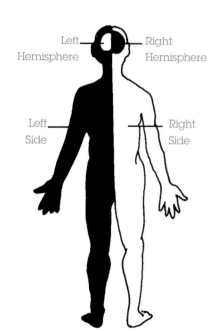

Left Hemisphere
Right Hemisphere

Left Side
Right Side

Characteristically, the left hemi patient retains good understanding of spoken language, expresses himself adequately and has good memory for events prior to injury. However, there are other problems that the speech pathologist may assist the patient with. Memory for new materials presented and events since injury may be impaired. The patient may have difficulty with time and place concepts. He may be unable to relate one event to another. Performance on physical activities as well as reading and writing may be marked by inconsistency and distractibility. Some patients may repeat a thought or physical motion over and over. This is called perseveration.

The left hemiplegic patient may experience visual perceptual problems or left aversion. Understanding the visual relationship of one object to another, realizing his own body position in space, organizing and sequencing visual stimuli and judging distances are typical visual perceptual problems a person with right hemisphere damage might experience. Left aversion or left ignoral refers to a patient's lack of awareness of his left side or the left side of objects. For example, he may bump into objects on his left side, comb only the right side of his hair, or eat food from just the right side of his plate.

Simple daily tasks, such as dressing and brushing the teeth, become difficult because of visual perceptual problems and the left aversion. Many left hemis have difficulty with reading, arithmetic and writing because they miss words and numbers on the page. It is necessary to teach the patient to be more aware of his visual perceptual deficits through practice and frequent repetition in order for him to compensate for these problems.

Some patients experience personality or behavioral changes. They may make excuses for their deficits. They may have less emotional control and become upset more easily (lability). Their ability for judgment, reasoning, problem solving and logical thinking may be reduced. In such cases, supervision of daily activities may be necessary. Attempts to reason with the patient may be futile and may lead to an extended argument. This can be upsetting to the patient and the family.

Awareness and understanding are primary in helping the patient compensate for his problems. Tasks aimed at increasing attention span, requiring the patient to attend to the left side of objects and fitting pieces together to make a whole are often helpful to the left hemiplegic. Frequent repetition and redirection may be necessary.

The person who has sustained damage to the left side of the brain, resulting in right-sided paralysis, is referred to as a right hemiplegic. Since speech and language are also controlled by the left side of the brain, the right hemiplegic is likely to have difficulties with speech and/or language.

Speech refers to the way sounds and words are formed by the coordination of breathing, voice and movement of the mouth, lips and tongue. When there is muscle weakness, paralysis and/or incoordination, speech will be distorted, slurred and difficult to understand. This is known as dysarthria.

Language refers to the way we learn words and their meanings and how we put them together to form sentences. We use language to communicate through talking, writing, reading and listening. Loss of this ability to use language is called *aphasia*. A person with right hemiplegia may also have a visual field cut, which means he cannot see on his right side. He must learn to turn his head until he sees a whole object. If this condition is present, try to approach the person from the left and keep things he needs on his good side.

Shunts, generally speaking, are devices to redirect the flow of fluids. With respect to the patient with brain injury, a shunt is surgically implanted plastic tubing that redirects the flow of cerebrospinal fluid (CSF). In certain situations, a shunt can prevent further brain injury when there is evidence of decreased reabsorption of CSF by the brain covering.

Villaret's Syndrome

Villaret's syndrome is defined as unilateral paralysis, characterized by paralysis of the superior constriction of the pharynx. Individuals with this syndrome experience difficulty in swallowing solids and suffer paralysis of the soft palate, paralysis of the vocal cords and loss of taste. They cannot speak.

Characteristics include: unilateral paralysis of the ninth, tenth, eleventh and twelfth cranial nerves and sometimes the seventh, due to a lesion in the retroparotid space, paralysis of the superior constriction of the pharynx and difficulty in swal-

The National Head Injury Foundation (NHIF) reports the number of brain injuries annually in the United States at 700,000. Automobile accidents account for 350,000 of these while falls and weapons are responsible for much of the remaining 50 percent. The number of deaths from brain injuries annually is 140,000. Annually, the number of brain injuries causing permanent disability is between 70,000 and 90,000. These injuries kill more Americans under the age of 34 than all other causes combined. Recent advances in medical and surgical care and technology have significantly increased the survival rate of traumatic brain-injured patients. Unfortunately, many of these people are left with both cognitive and physical impairments that require assistance for daily activities and recreational pursuits, including skiing.

lowing solids; paralysis of soft palate and fauces with anesthesia of these parts and of the pharynx; loss of taste in the posterior third of the tongue; paralysis of the vocal cords and anesthesia of the larynx; paralysis of the sternocleidomastoid and trapezius; and paralysis of the cervical sympathetic nerves (Horner's syndrome). Also called syndrome of retroparotid space.

Williams Syndrome

Williams syndrome was first described in 1961 by Dr. C.P. Williams of New Zealand. The syndrome is considered rare and occurs in about one in 20,000 births. The cause is presently unknown and cannot be detected before birth. Professionals trained in genetic disorders and birth defects can diagnose this syndrome after reviewing the child's history, performing a physical examination and observing the child's behavior. While no cure exists for Williams syndrome, the specific symptoms, developmental delays and behaviors can be treated or addressed.

Characteristics of Williams syndrome that directly affect skiing:

Physical Hyperacusis (bothered by loud noises)
Delayed developmental milestones (i.e., sitting, crawling, walking)
Poor balance and motor skills/extra loose or tight joints

Cognitive Meaningful memory for people and places
Fascination with spinning objects/short attention span
Poor fine motor skills/hyperactive behavior patterns
Spatial integration difficulties/learning disabilities

Social No fear of strangers/talkative nature
Prefers adults over peers/resistant to change/new ideas
Perseveration (especially on anticipated events)
Overly sensitive to feelings of others

General IQ 50–70/excels in verbal and reading/poor math skills
Poor sequential memory/heart anomalies
High calcium levels in blood/possible kidney concerns
Possible hernias/pixie-like facial features: wide eyes, puffy below eyes, wide mouth, small teeth widely spaced, small upturned nose

Skiers with disabilities take a variety of medications for a variety of needs. Below is a list of the more common medications used.

Analgesics

Primary effect	To relieve pain and discomfort
Examples	Narcotics: morphine, Dilaudid, Demerol, Percocet, Darvocet, Tylenol with codeine
	Non-narcotics (i.e., nonsteroidal antiinflammatory drugs, abbreviated NSAID): Toradol, Motrin, Naprosyn, Feldene, Tylenol, aspirin
Possible side effects	Respiratory depression, circulatory depression, nausea, constipation, drug dependency with potential for abuse

Antibacterial Medications

Furdantin	Given for urinary tract infection
Macrodantin	Side Effects: nausea, vomiting, diarrhea, dizziness, malaise
Septra	Given for urinary tract infections. It is a sulfa drug, not for persons allergic to sulfa
	Side Effects: Nausea, vomiting, headache, dizziness, allergic reaction

Antibiotics

Primary effect	To treat infections
Examples	Penicillin, ampicillin, amoxicillin, Septra, Bactrim, erythromycin, Ciprofloxicin, macrodantin and others
Possible side effects	Gastrointestinal complications (diarrhea), allergic reactions ranging from skin rashes to anaphylaxis

Anticholinergics

Primary effect	To control bladder spasm
Examples	Daricon, Ditropan, Cystospaz
Possible side effects	Dry mouth, constipation, blurred vision, urinary retention

Anticoagulants

Primary effect	To prevent and treat blood clots
Examples	Heparin, Coumadin
Possible side effects	Bleeding and bruising

Anticonvulsants

Primary effect	To control seizures
Examples	Dilantin, Tegretol, phenobarbitol, Depkane, Felbamate, Neurontin, Depokote, Valporic Acid, Clonopin
Possible side effects	Drowsiness/lethargy, decreased white blood cell count, gum overgrowth and bleeding, increased body hair (hirsutism)

Antidepressants

Primary effect	To control depression
Examples	Elavil, Pamelor, Tofranil, Norpramine, Prozac, Zoloft, Tranxene, Paxipan, Anaframil
Possible side effects	Drowsiness, confusion, anticholinergic side effects

Antiemetic Medications

Compazine	Given to control nausea and vomiting
	Side Effects: Drowsiness, abnormal movements

Medications that have been intensely tested and found to cause a desired effect against disease processes or abnormal body reactions. This is known as the medication's primary effect. Unfortunately, medications also cause unwanted reactions in individuals that are called side effects. The prescribed dose of a medication is the amount that maximizes the optimal desired effect and minimizes the unwanted side effects. Since individuals vary in their body size and metabolism, it is common for them to work with a physician and adjust the dose of a medication for their specific needs.

	Phenergan	Given for prevention and control of nausea and vomiting Side Effects: drowsiness, dizziness, dry mouth, blurred vision
	Vistaril	Given to control nausea and vomiting Side Effects: drowsiness, dry mouth
Antiinflammatory Medications	Decadron	Potent antiinflammatory effects in disorders of many organ systems Side Effects: fluid retention, potassium loss, muscle weakness, ulcers, abdominal distention, menstrual irregularities, suppression of growth in children
	Sulfasalazine	Given to reduce the intestinal inflammation of ulcerative colitis, used to treat rheumatoid arthritis Side Effects: rash, upset stomach, low blood count, sensitivity to strong sunlight, fatigue, dizziness, ringing in the ears, chills, nausea, abdominal pain, feeling of ill health
Antimalarial Medications	Plaquenil	Given to treat malaria, given in lupus and rheumatoid arthritis to decrease the symptoms Side Effects: possible damage to the retina (a part of the eye)
Anti-Parkinson's Medications	Levodopa	Given to relieve symptoms of Parkinson's disease, used to treat emotional incontinence, helpful for pain relief with shingles Side Effects: muscle spasms, inability to control some muscle groups, loss of appetite, nausea, dry mouth, difficulty eating, hand tremors, dizziness, numbness, confusion, mood changes
	Sinemet	Given to reduce the side effects of Levodopa Side Effects: loss of appetite, dry mouth, muscle spasms
Antispasmodic Medications	Primary effect	To control spasticity
	Examples	Balcofin (Lioresal), Dantrium, Valium
	Possible side effects	Drowsiness/lethargy, fatigue, liver damage
Gold Treatments	Myochrysine	Given to treat rheumatoid arthritis to slow down damage to cartilage and bone
	Solganal; Ridaura	Side Effects: rash, mouth sores, blood or protein in the urine, kidney damage, abnormal blood counts, nausea, hair loss, nail loss, gingivitis
H2 Blockers	Tagamet; Zantac; Prilosec	Given to treat or prevent ulcers Side Effects: headache, dizziness, constipation, diarrhea, rash, muscle aches

Hypertensive Medications	Aldactazide	A diuretic medication Side Effects: dry mouth, weakness, lethargy, drowsiness, muscle cramps, hypotension, gastrointestinal symptoms
	Apresoline	Given for reduction of high blood pressure Side Effects: continued malaise, chest pain, headache, nausea, vomiting, diarrhea, changes in the blood pressure
Immuno-suppressives	Imuran; Cyclosporin	Given for many autoimmune diseases to decrease overactivity of the immune system, used also in transplant patients so the body won't reject the new part Side Effects: increased risk of infection, lower blood counts, bleeding into the bladder, increased future risk of malignancy (cancer), possible liver or kidney damage
	Cytoxin; Methotrexate	Used as chemotherapy in high doses to treat various cancers, used in low doses in some autoimmune diseases to slow progression in cases where conventional medications are not effective Side Effects: gastrointestinal bleeding, high fever and chills, possible seizures, diarrhea, stomach pain, mouth sores, blood in the urine, shortness of breath, cough, swelling of legs and feet, yellow color of skin/eyes, lowered blood count, increased future risk of cancer, increased risk of infection, blood vessel inflammation
	Betaseron	Used to help decrease the number of attacks in multiple sclerosis and to lesson the severity of the attacks, and hopefully slow the progression of the disease Side Effects: flu-like symptoms (which may be severe, but usually disappear in a few weeks or months) that include high fever, chills, achy feeling, spots or discolorations at the sites of injection, depression (which may be severe enough to lead to possible suicide), increased risk of infection. This is a new drug and the long-term effects are as yet unknown.
Muscle Relaxants	Soma; Flexeril; Robaxin; Maolate	Used to relax muscles that are stiff or rigid from injury Used to relax muscles affected by neuromuscular diseases Side Effects: drowsiness, dry mouth, dizziness, fatigue, increased heart rate, nausea
Psycho-stimulants	Ritalin	Given to decrease hyperactivity and increase attention span in attention deficit disorder, used in narcolepsy (sleep seizure disorders) Side Effects: loss of appetite, sleep problems, lethargy
	Cylert	Given for attention deficit disorder to increase attention span and decrease hyperactivity, used to treat narcolepsy to decrease seizures, used to treat fatigue in diseases with chronic fatigue as a symptom Side Effects: sleeplessness, appetite loss, stomach ache, irritability, depression, nausea, headache, drowsiness
	Dexedrine	Used short-term for diet control, helpful with behavioral

problems in children, helps children with attention deficit disorder, used to treat narcolepsy
Side Effects: palpitations, restlessness, overstimulation, dizziness, sleeplessness, increased blood pressure, rapid heartbeat

Sedatives	Primary effect	To control anxiety and agitation
	Examples	Benzodiazepine: Valium, Ativan, Xanax, Transene
		Phenothiazine: Thorazine, Haldol
	Possible side effects	Drowsiness/lethargy, dizziness, drug tolerance, abnormal movements, increased temperature and muscular rigidity

| **Steroids (Corticosteroids)** | Prednisone; ACTH; Solu-Medrol | Given to decrease the severity and shorten the length of attacks in many diseases (e.g., autoimmune diseases) as well as to help slow the worsening of many diseases; used to decrease inflammation and swelling of many tissues, joints, organ systems, and other body parts
Side Effects: edema (swelling), muscle weakness, bone thinning, difficulty sleeping, agitation, upset stomach, mouth sores, depression, nervousness, irritability, infections that are hard detect, fast heartbeat, possible ulcers, gastrointestinal bleeding, increased blood sugar, growth of body hair |

Stool softeners	Primary effect	To maintain soft stool, regulate bowel function
	Examples	Colace, Pericolace, Dialose, Surfak
	Possible side effects	Diarrhea

TECHNICAL AND MECHANICAL FOUNDATIONS

The American Teaching System (ATS) is founded on four major technical and mechanical components: (1) the Skills Concept, (2) the Skiing Model and an appropriate set of Center Line images illustrating the Skiing Model (for use as a reference in developing lesson plans), (3) the relationship between biomechanics and the Skiing Model, and (4) the movement analysis techniques used to shape the learning experience. The following sections will define these components and the terminology used.

The Skills Concept

The concept that motor skills are basic building blocks is central to ATS. What is a skill? Fleishman (1972) defines skill as a "level of proficiency on a specific task or limited group of tasks." Ability, on the other hand, is thought to be a more basic characteristic that may be used in developing skills. Thus a specific skill is acquired through practice and experience, while the level of skill that may be attained depends primarily on a certain collection of abilities.

An understanding of the Skills Concept allows the instructor to develop lesson plans and adjust those plans as necessary to best help students progress. A rigid dependence on a set of maneuvers or a strict maneuver-based progression will interfere with learning and lead to frustration. Remember, you are teaching people, and each individual brings a different set of attributes to the sport at hand—different abilities, sports and movement experiences, and attitudes toward the learning situation. The principles on which to base the mechanics of your teaching, therefore, must be fundamental and adaptable to the variety of situations you will encounter.

A clear understanding of the Skills Concept and the related concept of ability is necessary because they apply to all of the skiing disciplines: alpine, nordic downhill, nordic cross-country, adaptive, and snowboard.

The value of introducing alternative movement progressions and changing the emphasis on particular movement patterns in a lesson is best determined by checking for skill development. The guiding principle is that the maneuvers you teach should provide building blocks for acquisition of skills. An exercise has value when it strengthens one or more of the basic skills.

There have been a number of changes in how the Skills Concept has been viewed in ATS since its initial introduction. Our current understanding of skills differs somewhat from the early descriptions in that all are now movement focused and the concept of control is integrated in the skills definitions. The four fundamental skills are as follows.

Balancing movements are the movements required to keep the body in equilibrium (either static or dynamic) when it is acted upon by external forces. These external forces may be the result of deliberate actions on the skier's part (turning the skis or adjusting edge angles), or they may result from reaction to disturbances (uneven snow surfaces or changes in terrain). The balancing movements may involve relatively gross body adjustments or almost imperceptible adjustments, depending on the circumstances.

Rotary movements are movements involving rotation, or a tendency toward rotation, of either the body as a whole or of one part of the body relative to another. As is the case with balancing movements, rotary movements may be subtle or quite strong, fully developed or blocked (tendency toward rotation), and active or reactive, depending on the situation and the skier's wishes. For efficiency and stability, it is generally desirable to use the lower body to generate rotary movements.

Edge-control movements are movements that affect the way the edges of the skis contact the snow surface. Instructors introduce the concept of "control" to the edging movements so students will clearly recognize that the forces that ultimately turn their skis come from the interaction between the skis and the snow and that the edges are the active interface between the skier and the snow.

Pressure-control movements are movements used to regulate and adjust the pressure the skis exert on the snow as they move on or through the snow.

Instructors need to elaborate on these fundamental skills and relate them directly to the events and actions that take place during turns. This must be done for all levels of skiing, from introductory to advanced levels. Whenever possible, descriptions of desired actions should be specific and refer to muscular movements that students can understand. In this way, fundamental skills become part of analyzing skier actions and giving specific skier instructions.

Actually, good skiing has a characteristic signature that allows definition of a useful model. The characteristic signature of good skiing shows rhythm, flow of movement, efficiency, power, sensitivity, and precision. These qualities serve as the departure point for defining the Skiing Model.

To be a universally valid model, it must be applicable to all levels of skiing (from beginner to expert) in all conditions (from groomed cruising slopes to extremes to racing) and to all age groups (from children to senior citizens). The qualities identified—rhythm, flow of movement, efficiency, power, sensitivity, and precision—do apply to all the variations encountered in skiing.

You must recognize that the maneuvers you teach are seldom ends in themselves. They are tools for overall skill enhancement and are representative of typical stages of skill development. Well-thought-out exercises and maneuvers should emphasize edge control, pressure control, and rotary movements of the legs and torso. They should also encourage students in learning to balance while moving across the surface of the snow. Keep in mind that there should be continuity in skill development so that exercises and maneuvers develop basic skills in a consistent manner from the beginning to the advanced level. Also remember that the central problem for the learner is how to balance while in motion and while performing the complicated muscular movements required to control the motion.

The Skiing Model and the Center Line

To anchor the technical and mechanical foundations, we needed to define the Center Line then serve as checkpoints during the suggested instructional progression. The majority of instruction is carried out at the lower levels, and the foundation established at these levels serves as the point of departure for skill development at the upper or expert levels. Consequently, the instructor should see the Center Line images demonstrated on groomed snow as an aid in focusing lesson plans. The objective is efficient and effective skiing under all terrain and snow conditions, and the instructor and student will usually operate in a mutual learning environment, with the basic characteristics of good skiing guiding their activities rather than any specific Center Line image. An important part of any lesson at the expert level is tactics (skill to define the Skiing Model). What are the components of such a model? They are, first, its qualities—the distinctive signature

described above. Next, there are the fundamental building blocks—the skills identified above. Then, there must be a prescription for using the building blocks when applying the model. Finally, there must be guidance for applying the fundamentals so both the student and the teacher clearly see the interrelationship of the various tasks and exercises used to improve the student's skiing.

To help focus the Skiing Model and provide structure, the concept of Center Line images has been introduced in ATS. (Center Line images have been identified for all the skiing disciplines.) The Center Line images serve as a reference when judging particular phases of skiing, a reference that helps both instructors and students evaluate the student's level of achievement at any stage of development.

The specific maneuvers that show progression from elementary skiing to high levels of proficiency make up the Center Line images and provide the reference (structure) instructors and students need. The selected maneuvers must be consistent in the way they showcase Fundamental Skills and form a logical progression from simple to complex movements. Plus, the image they convey must reflect the characteristic signature of good skiing. The specific maneuvers selected to define the Center Line then serve as checkpoints during the suggested instructional progression.

The majority of instruction is carried out at the lower levels, and the foundation established at these levels serves as the point of departure for skill development at the upper or expert levels. Consequently, the instructor should see the Center Line images demonstrated on groomed snow as an aid in focusing lesson plans. The objective is efficient and effective skiing under all terrain and snow conditions, and the instructor and student

will usually operate in a mutual learning environment, with the basic characteristics of good skiing guiding their activities rather than any specific Center Line image. An important part of any lesson at the expert level is tactics (skillful methods used to gain a desired objective).

Center Line images should not become the content of your lessons. We do not teach the Center Line, and our customers do not come to lessons with the personal goal of learning a specific Center Line maneuver. What we do teach are movements and movement patterns that provide students with a sound foundation that will ensure success in whatever skiing situation they may find themselves. In some cases, you will have students who wish to improve specific aspects of their skiing, such as carving, speed control, and linking turns. You can help students accomplish their goals while still developing the versatile skills base they need.

As instructors, we need to develop guidelines for applying the Fundamental Skills at each level of development. These guidelines should identify the common features of each skill for each level of the Center Line, as defined by the selected maneuvers. Furthermore, the guidelines should remain valid at the expert level to help evaluation of the effectiveness and efficiency of movements in any situation that may be encountered.

Biomechanics, the Skiing Model, and Skills

In reviewing skill definitions and the guidelines for applying the Skills Concept to skier development, it becomes apparent that the key concepts are all biomechanical. There are the movements themselves, control of the movements, the characterization of the movements, the effects of differing movements, and the shaping of movements as the skill levels progress from beginning to expert. Thus, a deeper understanding of the Skills Concept and the appropriate Skiing Model to use as a reference requires looking at the biomechanics involved.

Traditionally, when instructors have encountered biomechanics, their reaction has been, "Oh no, not that incomprehensible, esoteric stuff about vectors, forces, Newton's laws, and who knows what else! Why can't we just keep it simple and talk about ski technique instead?" Yet discussions of ski technique are often based on some interpretation of the underlying mechanics and what is going on with the body and skis, even if the term "biomechanics" is not actually used. Not only is this true in discussions of technique, it is even more evident in clinics on "movement analysis" or "error recognition/error correction."

First, let us define what we mean by biomechanics. The term itself is a composite and a relatively recent addition to the English language (you will not find the term in a 1960 edition of Webster's, for example). The term today means the study of living creatures in motion, in particular, humans in motion. In the 1970s and early 1980s, biomechanics was primarily involved with measurements and some limited modeling to predict human motor variables that cannot be measured directly. In the 1990s, the focus has shifted to issues of motor control in human movement. Today, the goal of the study of biomechanics and motor control is to assess and understand

human movement. This goal is becoming more realizable as a result of progress in our understanding of the basic physics involved, advances in modem computing technology, measurement and measurement processing technology, and our understanding of how muscles work.

Certainly one approach to biomechanics in skiing is to base all analysis on the traditional Newtonian approach used in engineering and physics. That is, start with the identification of all the forces acting on the skier and/or skis, draw appropriate diagrams that display how and where these forces act on the skier and/or skis, and then analyze the situation after deciding which motion to study. This approach is quite complicated since a reference frame must be identified and all forces must be expressed in the selected reference frame. Furthermore, the forces involved are all continuously changing in time and the body-generated forces may be the result of different muscular actions, many of which produce the same overall effect. The situation rapidly becomes quite confusing, even for individuals trained in the analysis of dynamic systems. The usual temptation is to assume some simplified model or to identify what one believes to be a key characteristic of the situation and then build the analysis based on these assumptions. This approach is sometimes useful; sometimes it merely confirms something one knows from experience; or more often, it leads to erroneous conclusions.

An alternative approach suggests itself when we realize that the primary help we can derive from biomechanics is a guide to our thinking about the effectiveness and efficiency of movements for selected tasks. After all, if a skier intends to make a turn in some direction, does something with the body and the skis, and the change in direction takes place, then there is nothing

wrong with the movements used. What an instructor needs to be concerned with are the qualities of the movements involved. Were they as effective or efficient as they could have been? Did they feel good and look good? The previously identified characteristics of good skiing all focus on the qualities of the turns and movements, not on whether a turn actually happened. Granted, the first concern of students is whether they can make the turn where and when they want to. Once that happens, however, the value of instruction is in shaping the qualities of the turns and extending the range of conditions in which students can use the turns they know how to make. The quality of motion, in fact, is what we are judging when we look at someone skiing, whether in a certification setting, a teaching situation, or just casual observation on the slope.

When judging quality of movements, first consider the issue of efficiency. Efficiency is clearly related to the expenditure of energy necessary to accomplish a given task. Energy expenditure is a much easier concept to deal with than detailed analysis of forces as in the Newtonian approach. Body language clearly signals whether someone is working hard; and, even without the benefit of biomechanics, everyone has an intuitive feeling that jerky, harsh movements with visible tension are not efficient. The ATS Skiing Model captures this distinction in the descriptions of what makes a movement efficient by using terms such as "flowing," "smooth," "guiding," "continuous flow," and so on.

This view is supported by the current thoughts in biomechanics research. A decade ago, very little was being done regarding the study of energy involved in human movement. Now, the focus is on the "human motors" themselves as generators, absorbers, and transferors of energy. The sources of energy that need to be managed in the context of skiing are the energy derived from gravity (energy given to us by the lifts that raise us in the gravitational field), the energy available in our bodies (metabolism), and the energy available in skiing equipment as a result of deformation of the materials. We can judge quality of motion by how we manage the energy available to us in accomplishing our skiing goals, whether these are minimum time in a race or maximum enjoyment from a full day on the mountain. Recreational skiing, like any other motion sport, is enjoyable partly because of the sensation of speed and the control of motion. Smooth, seemingly effortless movements give the most satisfaction.

What are the causes of inefficient movements? The most obvious is when extensors (the muscles that straighten body parts) and flexors (the muscles that contract body parts) work in opposition. This is known as co-contraction in the biomechanics field. The muscles are, essentially, fighting each other to produce some net movement, resulting in a high expenditure of energy. This type of activity occurs most often when an individual feels the need to stabilize the body while performing some movement. This is felt as tension in different body segments during a run. To feel how this enters your own skiing, focus on how much relaxation you can achieve between turns or on which muscles are working during a particular turn. Note the difference as you move from the groomed snow to garbage to bumps.

Another cause of inefficiency is isometric contraction against the force of gravity. In ATS, this cause is addressed through stance and the way the body's center of mass moves during turns. While the term "stance" usually implies a static position, in skiing the body is rarely completely at rest. Stance is used in ATS to describe the reference or neutral position from

which movements are initiated or to which a skier returns after execution of a particular sequence of movements. The preferred mechanism for reacting to gravity (as well as other forces that arise during skiing) is to use skeletal alignment and not the muscles. A somewhat more subtle point is that any time a limb is held in a stationary position during motion, it is more than likely doing work against the force of gravity in addition to whatever else is going on.

An additional cause of inefficiency, closely related to co-contraction, occurs when the energy generated at one joint is absorbed at another. This is a bit difficult to visualize, but often happens during alternating limb movements. For example, this occurs in normal walking during the double support phase when the energy increase of the push-off leg takes place at the same time that the weight-accepting leg absorbs energy. It is obvious that this type of activity needs to happen—the basic mechanics of the biped walking task require such movements. The efficiency of the event, however, is determined by just how the movement is executed. An individual should expend no more energy than is absolutely necessary for the task.

The last major cause of inefficiency in movement is the relative smoothness or jerkiness of the movement. Smooth movement is characterized by continuous interchanges of limb energy. Jerky movements consist of a succession of stops and starts. Each of these bursts of energy generation and absorption has a metabolic cost; therefore, jerky movements are inefficient.

Another area where energy considerations can be examined without getting all tangled up in the perils of detailed mechanical analysis is in the analysis of turns, specifically the efficiency and effectiveness of turns. Instructors spend a lot of time discussing turn

shape and how different movements influence turn shape. The real issue, however, is what the purpose of the turn or series of turns is to be and what is pertinent to attaining that purpose. Simply put, the primary purpose of any turn is to change the direction of travel of the skier down the mountain. The change in direction may also serve to reduce speed if speed control is one of the goals. To satisfy this purpose, any movement that results in the desired change of direction is correct; however, particular qualities are usually demanded, and these can radically change the mechanics involved. Everything from racing to recreational skiing in any conditions is included in an examination of the effectiveness and efficiency of turns.

To understand how to judge the efficiency of ski turns, the concepts of mechanical work and energy must be considered. In essence, efficiency is an energy management game. For example, if you want to be the fastest down the race course, you need to be careful of how and where your energy is lost. The recreational skier may wish to use the turns to slow down, so where and how the energy is lost also will be of interest in that case. The ATS Skiing Model focuses on the concept of continuous flow of movement, a concept that is directly tied to where in the turns you scrub speed and what the results are on the movement of your center of mass. If the changes are not smooth, then it is likely your body reactions will not be smooth either. And, as mentioned before, jerky movements are inefficient.

Considerable insight into the mechanics of skiing can be gained from thinking about energy without getting too involved with the details of mechanics. For some purposes, we do need to think about forces in detail and how those forces originate and are applied. For example, when analyzing the sequence of movements that take place in a given turn, we need to consider how movements are initiated and what happens thereafter.

The study of biomechanics and mechanical analysis of motor sports requires an understanding of basic physics and anatomy. Such material is beyond the scope of this manual, but will be available in future PSIA publications.

Movement Analysis

As an instructor, you will be spending considerable time either doing movement analysis or discussing it, certainly as part of certification examinations. Often this topic will arise in the context of "error recognition" or "error correction." Since ATS promotes a nonjudgmental, humanistic, teaching/learning environment, the focus is better placed on "movement analysis." "Error" is not a nonjudgmental term. (Similar considerations hold for discussions of "bad habits.") If a student has never had a lesson but has experimented with skiing alone (or been instructed by well-meaning but nonprofessional friends), he or she will have developed many ineffective or inefficient movements. Your task as a teacher is to show the student there is a better way without attaching a negative judgment to what he or she already knows.

Trained physical educators study kinesiology (the study of muscles and their movements) to better understand the elements of physical performance and to be able to teach motor sports. One of the best texts in this area is *Kinesiology* by Logan and McKinney (Brown Co. Publ., 1972). A key point the authors make is that "teaching neuromuscular skills is based on

(1) the analytical ability of the physical educator and (2) the ability to communicate pertinent facts of skill analyses to learners. Analysis is the beginning point for teaching."

They also note that a lot of analysis in teaching motor sports is done visually, after only a cursory (often onetime) observation of the performance, with immediate feedback to the student. Experienced instructors know enough to restrain themselves from instant analysis and feedback, but the inexperienced often engage in "instant teaching" because they feel they must do something or else the students may think no instruction is taking place. A valid analysis of what is causing difficulties in a given individual's riding may require many runs and observations. Better yet, a video camera may be used so that specific movement patterns can be isolated and viewed repeatedly. (Exercise caution in the use of video, however, as it may interfere with a student's learning.)

Even though much has been written in the physical education field since 1972, Logan and McKinney's suggested sequence for movement analysis still forms the basis for the most practical and sound approach. They propose a segmental approach to observing sports skills in visual as well as cinematic analysis. Their suggested sequence for analysis is as follows: (1) the total performance, (2) pelvic area and the rib cage, (3) base of support or feet, (4) head and shoulders, (5) arms and hands, (6) knees and hips, (7) follow-through, and (8) the total performance again. For skiing, follow-through (the movement of the body or limbs after the release

of a thrown object) is not an important feature.

Furthermore, the preferred sequence of observation for skiing is: (1) the total performance, (2) pelvic area and the rib cage, (3) knees and hips, (4) base of support or feet, (5) head and shoulders, (6) arms and hands, and (7) the total performance again. Clearly, no one will be able to observe all of the above in one trial or even a few turns. When performing movement analysis, however, you need to have a clear purpose in mind (what you are trying to learn from the observations and analysis) and a clear plan for observation (how you are going to observe the student's performance).

One additional point, when we discuss technical issues, such as precisely what information movement analysis provides and how we should use it, we need to keep the audience clearly in mind. The information needs of the instructor and the student are clearly different. Unless asked to elaborate further, keep the discussion simple for students. For instructors, be certain of your understanding before starting a technical discussion. Remember that for students your goals should be to improve their effectiveness, efficiency and understanding of what the movement options are in different situations.

* Excerpts reprinted with permission of the Professional Ski Instructors of America from *Strategies for Teaching: American Teaching System*, P.S.I.A., Publishers Press, Salt Lake City, Utah. © 1987 and *American Teaching System: Alpine Skiing*, P.S.I.A., © 1993.

Hal's Pals

HAL'S PALS began in 1983 as "Bestfriends," a group of dolls with disabilities originated by Audrey Boxwell and Susan Anderson of Fraser, Colorado. Since that time, HAL'S PALS have become recognized and endorsed by experts who work with diverse disabilities, and have appeared in national and international print and broadcast media.

Hal O'Leary was the inspiration for the HAL doll, the signature piece of HAL'S PALS. The dolls with disabilities have an appealing appearance and cheerful attitude and demonstrate a variety of "can do" challenges. Because the PALS are dolls, children are not threatened when PALS are used to demonstrate information about specific disabilities. The identification of a child with disabilities with these role models reinforces self-esteem and raises expectations. The conversations about disabilities that the dolls encourage help to remove "disabling barriers" and teach disability awareness to all children—those with and without disabilites.

HAL'S PALS can be found in homes, hospitals, rehabilitation centers and kindergarten-to-college classrooms. The PALS are used for fund-raisers by a variety of national disability organizations and downhill skiing groups.

The product line is expanding to include new additions for classroom use and specially adapted toys. To determine availability in your area, call 303-726-5400 or write to: HAL'S PALS, P.O. Box 3490, Winter Park, CO 80482.

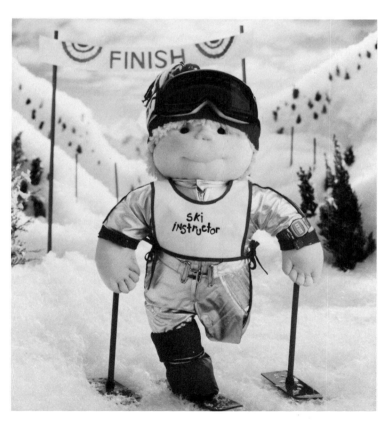

SOURCE SUSAN ANDERSON

National Handicapped Sports Chapters

ALABAMA

Alabama Handicapped Sportsmen
11802 Creighton Ave.
Northport, AL 35476
(205) 339-2800

ALASKA

Alpine Alternatives
2518 East Tudor Rd., Ste . 105
Anchorage, AK 99507
(907) 561-6655

Challenge Alaska
P.O. Box 110065
Anchorage, AK 99511-0065
(907) 563-2658

Access Alaska
3710 Woodland Dr., Ste. 900
Anchorage, AK 99517-2564

ARIZONA

Mesa Association of Sports
for the Disabled
P.O. Box 4727
Mesa, AZ 85211-4727
(602) 649-2258

CALIFORNIA

NHS of Southern California
"The Unrecables"
P.O. Box 24856
Los Angeles, CA 90024
(310) 374-6775

NHS of Orange County
531 Heather Ave.
La Habra, CA 90631
(310) 697-0351

San Diego Adventurers
3169 Winlow St.
San Diego, CA 92105
(619) 582-3871

California Handicapped Skiers
P.O. Box 2897
Big Bear Lake, CA 92315-2897
(714) 585-2519, ext. 269

Mother Lode Chapter
P.O. Box 4274
Camp Connell, CA 95223
(209) 795-5288

NHS, Northern California Chapter
5932 Illinois Ave.
Orangevale, CA 95662
(916) 989-0402

NHS, Northern California Chapter
Tahoe Handicapped Ski School
P.O. Box 9780
Truckee, CA 95737
(916) 581-4161

COLORADO

Golf 4 Fun
P.O. Box 5304
Englewood, CO 80155
(303) 985-5851

Rocky Mountain Handicapped
Sportsmen's Association
P.O. Box 18036, Capital Hill Station
Denver, CO 80218
(303) 934-9540

Front Range Sports
5556 Wheeling St.
Denver, CO 80239
(303) 373-0452

Eldora Special Recreation Program
P.O. Box 19016
Boulder, CO 80308-9016
(303) 442-0606

Breckenridge Outdoor Educ. Center
P.O. Box 697
Breckenridge, CO 80424
(303) 453-6422

Nat'l Sports Center for the Disabled
P.O. Box 36
Winter Park, CO 80482
(303) 726-5514

Crested Butte Physically Challenged
Skier Program
P.O. Box A
Crested Butte, CO 81225

Durango/Purgatory Adaptive
Sports Association
P.O. Box 1884
Durango, CO 81301
(303) 259-0374

Colorado Discover Ability
P.O. Box 3444
Grand Junction, CO 81502
(303) 268-5573

Aspen Handicapped Skiers Assn.
P.O. Box 5429
Snowmass Village, CO 81615
(303) 923-3294

Southern Colorado Center for
Challenged Athletes
1124 S. Russett Dr.
Pueblo West, CO 81007
(719) 549-3330

CONNECTICUT

Connecticut Handicapped Ski
Foundation
599 Graham Rd.
South Windsor, CT 06074
(203) 644-1322

DC, MARYLAND, NORTH VIRGINIA

National Ocean Access Project
P.O. Box 33141, Farragut Station
Washington, DC 20033
(301) 217-9843

Baltimore Adaptive Recreational Sports
301 Washington Ave.
Towson, MD 21204
(410) 887-5370

Chesapeake Region Accessible Boating
P.O. Box 6564
Annapolis, MD 21401-0564
(301) 974-2628

Nation's Capital Handicapped Sports
P.O. Box 220254
Chantilly, VA 22022-0254
(202) 234-6275

FLORIDA

Physically Adapted Recr. & Sports
P.O. Box 16406
Jacksonville, FL 32245-6406
(904) 399-6884

NHS, South Florida Chapter
P.O. Box 831535
Miami, FL 33183-1535
(305) 444-6104

GEORGIA

NHS, Atlanta Chapter
P.O. Box 327
Clarkson, GA 30021
(404) 498-7204

IDAHO

Recreation Unlimited, Inc.
P.O. Box 447
Boise, ID 83701
(208) 336-3293

ILLINOIS

Chicagoland Handicapped Skiers
1086 Briarcliffe
Wheaton, IL 60187
(708) 682-4018

Jed Goldman Adaptive Sailing Prog.
425 E. McFetridge Dr.
Chicago, IL 60605
(312) 294-2270

RIC-Skiers Rehab. Institute of Chicago
345 E. Superior St.
Chicago, IL 60611
(312) 908-4292

INDIANA

Greater Indianapolis Hnd. Skiing
C/o Indiana Pacers
Director of Community Relations
300 E. Market St.
Indianapolis, IN 46204
(317) 924-7059

Special Outdoor Leisure
  Opportunities, Inc. (S.O.L.O.)
P.O. Box 6221
South Bend, IN 46660
(219) 259-6172

Calumet Region Chapter
P.O. Box 717
East Chicago, IN 46712
(219) 392-9604

IOWA

Sundown Handicapped Skiers
Sundown Ski Area
9000 Asbury Rd.
Dubuque, IA 52001
(319) 582-7939

KANSAS

Adaptive Sports & Recreation of Topeka
2501 S.E. Michigan
Topeka, KS 66605
(913) 233-1961

MAINE

Maine Handicapped Skiing
Sunday River Ski Resort
RR 2, Box 1971
Bethel, ME 04217-9600
(207) 824-2440

Maine Accessible Adventures
52 Deane St.
Gardiner, ME 40345
(207) 582-4730

MASSACHUSETTS, RHODE ISLAND

New England Handicapped Sportsmen's
  Association
26 McFarlin Rd.
Chelmsford, MA 01824
(508) 256-3240

Community Boating, Inc.
21 Embankment Rd.
Boston, MA 02114
(617) 523-1038

Courageous Sailing Center
1 First Ave., Charlestown Navy Yard
Parris Building
Charlestown, MA 02129
(617) 725-3263

MICHIGAN

Great Lakes Sailing Association
  for the Physically Disabled
150 W. Jefferson, Ste. 900
Detroit, MI 48220
(313) 225-7067

Michigan Handicapped Sports &
  Recreation Assn.
238 Woodview Ct., Apt. 244
Rochester Hills, MI 48307-4191
(313) 853-0648

Cannonsburg Challenged Ski Assn.
10831 Grange N.E.
Sparta, MI 49345-9451
(616) 887-4905

MINNESOTA

American Sledge Hockey Assn.
10933 Johnson Ave. S.
Bloomington, MN 55437
(612) 881-2129

Courage Alpine Skiers
3915 Golden Valley Rd.
Golden Valley, MN 55422
(612) 520-0495

Courage Center/Twin Port Flyers
205 W. 2nd St., #451
Duluth, MN 55802
(218) 727-6874

MONTANA

I Am Third Foundation–Eagle Mount
6901 Goldenstein Lane
Bozeman, MT 59715
(406) 586-1781

I Am Third Foundation
Dba Eagle Mt.–Great Falls
4237 2nd Ave. North
Great Falls, MT 59401
(406) 454-1449

I Am Third Foundation
Dba Eagle Mt.–Billings
P.O. Box 20233
Billings, MT 59401
(406) 245-5422

Dream Disabled Ski Program
P.O. Box 8300
Kalispell, MT 59903-1058
(406) 758-5411

Beyond Barriers
1900 Brooks, Ste. 115
Missoula, MT 59801
(406) 549-9878

NEVADA
NHS, Lakeside Chapter
749 Veterans Memorial Dr.
Las Vegas, NV 89101
(702) 229-6297

Northern Nevada Ski School
for the Disabled
P.O. Box 6244
Incline Village, NV 89450
(702) 832-0480

NEW HAMPSHIRE
NHS, Loon Mountain
55 Washington Ave.
Boston, MA 02152
(603) 745-8111, ext. 5663

North Passage
P.O. Box 127
Durham, NH 03824
(603) 862-0070

NEW MEXICO
The Adaptive Ski Program
2425 Ridgecrest Dr. SE
Albuquerque, NM 87108
(505) 262-7563

Challenge New Mexico
1570 Pacheco St., #E-6
Santa Fe, NM 87501-3937
(505) 988-7621

NEW YORK
Adolescent Sarcoma Patients'
Intensive Rehabilitation with
Exercise (A.S.P.I.R.E.)
196 E. 75th St.
New York, NY 10021
(212) 639-6713

A.S.P.I.R.E.–Glenville
123 Saratoga Rd.
P.O. Box 121
Glenville, NY 12302
(518) 437-9416

Sea Legs
88 Kelvin Ave.
Staten Island, NY 10306
(718) 987-6837

National Amputee Summer
Sports Assn., Ltd.
215 W. 92nd St., Ste. 15A
New York, NY 10025
(212) 874-4138

Disabled Ski Prog. at Ski Windham
EPSIA Educational Foundation
1-A Lincoln Ave.
Albany, NY 12205-4900
(518) 452-6095

Hunter Mt. Disabled Ski Program
P.O. Box 433
Hunter, NY 12442
(518) 263-4278

Loundsbury Ski Program
P.O. Box 370
Ellicottville, NY 14731
(716) 699-2345

Greek Peak Sports for the Disabled
508 Verna Dr.
Endwell, NY 13760
(607) 785-6960

OHIO
Great Lakes Amputee Athletic Assoc.
P.O. Box 617
Pemberville, OH 43450
(419) 287-4531

Three Trackers of Ohio
1542 Prospect Ave.
Rocky River, OH 44116
(216) 356-0987

OREGON
Flying Outriggers Ski Club
320 SW Stark, Ste. 211
Portland, OR 97204-2672
(503) 222-1327

Shared Outdoor Adventure Recreation
P.O. Box 14583
Portland, OR 97204-2672
(503) 238-1613

PENNSYLVANIA
Three Rivers Adaptive Sports
P.O. Box 38235
Pittsburgh, PA 15238
(412) 749-2281

Deutsch Institute
615 Jefferson Ave.
Scranton, PA 18510
(717) 348-1968

Philadelphia Area Handicapped
Skiing Club
4318 Spruce St.
Philadelphia, PA 19003
(215) 222-6277

TENNESSEE
Sports, Arts & Recr. of Chattanooga
Chattanooga State Tech CC, Rm. F50
4501 Amnicola Hwy.
Chattanooga, TN 37406
(615) 697-4473

TEXAS
Paraplegics on Independent
Nature Trips (P.O.I.N.T.)
4144 North Central Expwy., #515
Dallas, TX 75204
(214) 827-7404

Disabled Sports Assoc. of N. Texas
3810 W. Northwest High., Ste. 205
Dallas, TX 75220
(214) 352-4100

Southwest Wheelchair Athletic Assn.
1475 W. Gray, Ste. 161
Houston, TX 77019
(713) 522-9769

Houston Area Chapter, NOAP
1500 F.M. 2094, Box 611
Kemah, TX 77565
(714) 334-1993

UTAH

Utah Handicapped Skiers Assoc.
P.O. Box 543
Roy, UT 84067-0543
(801) 777-7029

National Ability Center
P.O. Box 680286
Park City, UT 84068-0286
(801) 649-3991

VERMONT

Vermont Handicapped Ski
    & Sports Assn.
P.O. Box 261
Brownsville, VT 05037
(802) 484-3525

VIRGINIA

Richmond Athletes with
    Disabilities Sports
P.O. Box 311
Richmond, VA 23202-9998
(804) 747-7769

Southern Chesapeake Adaptive
    Maritime Program
P.O. Box 62567
Virginia Beach, VA 23466
(804) 463-8649

WASHINGTON

Footloose Sailing Association
2319 N. 45th St., #142
Seattle, WA 98103
(206) 632-3622

Seattle Handicapped Sports &
    Recreation Assoc.
8034 Forest Dr. NE
Seattle, WA 98105
(206) 526-1633

Team USABLE
P.O. Box 4124
Bellingham, WA 98227
(206) 671-5771

WEST VIRGINIA

The Challenged Athletes of
    Silver Creek, West Virginia
1 Silver Creek Pkwy.
Snowshoe, WV 26291
(304) 339-6538

CANADA

Operation Able/Sail
P.O. Box 842
Moncton, NB E1C 8H7
Canada
(506) 857-3988

National Organizations

The 52 Association for the
    Handicapped, Inc.
350 5th Ave.
New York, NY 10188
(212) 563-9797

American Athletic Association
    for the Deaf (AAAD)
3916 Lantern Drive
Silver Spring, MD 20902

Amputee Sports Association
P.O. Box 14663
Savannah, GA 31404
(912) 355-8333

Blind Outdoor Leisure
    Development (BOLD)
533 E. Main St.
Aspen, CO 81611

Braille Sports Foundation
7525 North St.
Minneapolis, MN 55426
(612) 935-0423, (612) 920-9363

Breckenridge Outdoor Education
    Center (BOEC)
P.O. Box 697
Breckenridge, CO 80424
(303) 453-6422

Colorado State Library Services for
    the Blind and Physically Handicapped
1313 Sherman St.
Denver, CO 80203
1-800-332-5852

Handicapped Sports Program
Children's Hospital
1056 E. 19th Ave.
Denver, CO 80218
(303) 861-6590

Healthsports, Inc.
2455 W. Lake St.
Minneapolis, MN 55408

Horizons for the Handicapped
325 7th Street
Steamboat Springs, CO 80477
(303) 879-4466

International Sports Organization
   for the Disabled (ISOD)
Secretariat CMSH82
CH-1861
Les Mosses, Switzerland

National Association of Sports
   for Cerebral Palsied (NASCP)
66 E. 34th St.
New York, NY 10016

National Handicapped Sports
451 Hungerford Dr., Ste. 100
Rockville, MD 20850
(301) 217-0960 Telephone
(301) 217-0960 Telefax

National Organization on Disabilities
910 16th St., NW, Ste. 600
Washington, DC 20006
(202) 293-5960

National Wheelchair Athletic
   Association (NWAA)
660 Capitol Bldg.
301 7th Ave. N.
Nashville, TN 37129

Regional Mobility
401 Linden Center Dr.
Fort Collins, CO 80524
(303) 484-3800

United Cerebral Palsy Association
Sports Coordinator
Penn Plaza, Ste. 804
New York, NY 10001
(212) 268-6655

United States Association of
   Blind Athletes (USABA)
55 W. California Ave.
Beach Haven, NJ 08008

United States Deaf Skiers Association
(USDSA)
5159 Davis Ave.
Hackensack, NJ 07601

United States Disabled Ski Team
P.O. Box 100
Park City, UT 84060

United States Olympic Committee
1 Olympic House
Colorado Springs, CO 80909-5760

Pat Kayser and Emily Quinn, accomplished
sit skier   PHOTO: JEANNE SMITH

"And then there is the fun, growth, smiles,
self-worth, confidence and risk-taking that our
students experience ... and so much more."

Publications

This is a very partial list from among many specialty handicap publications.

Ability, Majestic Press, Inc., P.O. Box 5311 Mission Hills,CA 91345. (818) 366-1552. Subscription: four issues per year.

Accent on Living, Raymond C. Cheever, Publisher, P.O. Box 700, Bloomington, IL 61702. (309) 378-2961. Subscription: four issues per year.

A Basic Course in Sign Language, by Tom Humphries, Carol Padden and Terence J. O'Rourke. T.J. Publishers, Inc., 817 Silver Spring Ave., Silver Spring, MD 20910. 1980.

American Teaching System: Alpine Skiing. P.S.I.A. 133 S. Van Gordon St., Lakewood, CO 80228. (303) 987-9390. $24.95 for members, $49.95 for nonmembers, plus tax, shipping and handling.

Careers & The Handicapped Magazine, Equal Opportunity Publications, Inc., 44 Broadway, Greenlawn, NY 11740. (516) 261-8899. Subscription: two issues per year.

Challenged American, The National Newspaper for the Disabled, Loy & Loy Communications, P.O. Box 4310, Sunland, CA 91041. Subscription: published every other month.

Mainstream, Exploding Myths, Inc., 2973 Beech St., San Diego, CA 92102. (619) 234-3138. Subscription: ten issues per year.

Palaestra, published in cooperation with the United States Olympic Committee's Committee on Sports for the Disabled. Challenge Publications Ltd., P.O. Box 508, Macomb, IL 61455. (309) 833-1902. Subscription: four issues per year.

A Positive Approach, CTEC 1600 Malone St., Municipal Airport, Millville, NJ 80332. (609) 327-4040. Subscription: six issues per year.

Regional Mobility, Regional Mobility Ltd., 401 Linden Center Dr., Ft. Collins, CO 80524. (303) 484-3800. Subscription: 11 issues per year.

Skiing by the Physically Handicapped, by Martin H. Krag, M.D. and Duane G. Messner, M.D. Clinics in Sports Medicine, Vol. 1, No. 2, July 1982. Department of Orthopaedics and Rehabilitation, University of Vermont College of Medicine, Given Building, Burlington, VT 05045.

Skiwee Games Manual, by Maggie Sjostrom and Christi Mueller Northrop, 1990. A program for children's instruction.

Spinal Network (news journal/resource directory for spinal cord injured). Spinal Network, P.O. Box 4162, Boulder, CO 80306. 1-800-338-5412.

Sports for the Leg Amputee, by Bernice Kegel, R.P.T. Medic Publishing Co., P.O. Box 89, Redmond, WA 98073. (206) 881-2883.

Sports 'n Spokes, the Magazine for Wheelchair Sports and Recreation, 5201 N. 19th Ave., Ste. 111, Phoenix, AZ 85015. Subscription: 12 issues per year.

Strategies for Teaching: American Teaching System, P.S.I.A. 133 S. Van Gordon St., Lakewood, CO 80228. (303) 987-9390. $5 per copy for members, $10 for nonmembers, plus tax, shipping and handling.

Videos and Films

Video on the self-loading monoski for rent or purchase from: Enabling Technologies, 2411 N. Federal Blvd., Denver, CO 80211.

"Reach for Fitness," by Richard Simmons, exercise for the physically challenged. Karl-Lorimar Home Video, 17942 Cowan, Irvine, CA 92714.

PSIA Videos

American Teaching System, Volume I

American Teaching System, Volume II

Alpine Sking

Fundamentals of Downhill Skiing

P.S.I.A., 133 S. Van Gordon St., Lakewood, CO 80228. (303) 987-9390.

NHS Videos

Adaptive Ski Teaching Mehods: A Practical Approach for Instructors

The Adaptive Teaching Video

NHS, 451 Hungerford Dr., Ste. 100 Rockville, MD 20850. (301) 217-0960.

FFS-Dual Ski
Mountain Man Industries
720 Front St.
Bozeman, MT 59715
(406) 587-0310

Mono Skis and Outriggers
Spokes 'N Motion
2225 S. Platte River Dr. W.
Denver, CO 80223
(303) 922-0605

Mono Skis Bi Unique, Bi Ski, and Superlight Outriggers
Enabling Technologies
Design/Manufacturer
2225 S. Platte River Dr.
Denver, CO 80223
(303) 936-0235

Shadow Mono Ski
Quickie Designs, Inc./Shadow Products
2842 Business Park Ave.
Fresno, CA 93727
(800) 456-8165

Outriggers
Ski Doctor
609 Monroe St.
Sacramento, CA 95825
(916) 488-5398
FAX: (916) 488-5397

Ski Harness
Steve Sanches
3603 Eliot
Denver, CO 80211
(303) 433-1434

Ski Bras
SKI EZE
4401 Devonshire
Lansing, MI 48910
(517) 882-4608

Yetti Ski
Radventures
20755 SW 238th Pl.
Sherwood, OR 97140
(503) 628-2895

Skistar Technologies
Milty's Bi-Ski
P.O. Box 7461
Tahoe City, CA 96145
(916) 581-2441

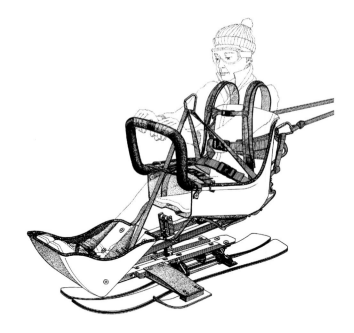

The FFS-Dual Ski from Mountain Man features adjustable fixed outriggers and air-shock absorber and handlebar. Adapts to standard skis for more advanced skiers.

Paul Spaight demos bi ski from Enabling Technologies.

**Notes from a
Volunteer**

For the first 12 winters that the Three Track Ski Club of Denver came to Winter Park, I participated as a volunteer ski instructor and chaperone with the group. At that time this was a small group of handicapped children and adults who came up to Winter Park from Children's Hospital. These first years of the program were exciting ones, for there was a pioneer spirit about them.

Each person who comes to volunteer his or her services to any group brings unique abilities and talent, along with a special wish to serve. I am an experienced ski instructor and a physical therapist, a good combination for this task. Consequently, it was an especially interesting and challenging experience for me—one that I cherished.

John Borelli and a volunteer.

As is always the case when one steps forward to become involved, I gained more than I gave. I usually had a small group of students, some children and some adults. The first objective was safety, the second fun, the third learning to ski. Somehow the third is always realized if the first two are taking place. And we did have such fun, I more than most.

One should never make generalizations about any group. Yet there are a few characteristics of handicapped people, both children and adults, that stand out in my mind. Most particularly these courageous individuals are eager to step out and take chances. There is heightened zest and appreciation for life, a joy of accomplishment. There is a thankful spirit toward those who are helping that makes a volunteer feel very special indeed.

We met some unique challenges:
How do you teach someone to get up when he or she falls down when:
  1. She has paralyzed arms and stomach muscles?
  2. She has two artificial legs and two outriggers?
  3. He has no legs and is skiing with a pelvic bucket and two outriggers?
How do you ride a chairlift alone in these circumstances, for the importance of independence is great?

How do you combine the need for safety with the desire for that same independence? We had some heartbreaking times, when some of those beloved members of the group who had lost limbs to cancer finally succumbed to the disease. Yet even during the hard times, there was an uplifting emphasis on life, living and especially on loving.

Volunteering with the program has been one of the highlights of my life. I recommend it to all of you who feel the call to do so. You will be part of an area of endeavor that will surpass ordinary living and add immeasurable value to your life, and to the lives of others.

Katie Branch